'One hell of a story'
DANIEL JAMES BROWN, AUTHOR OF 'THE BOYS IN THE BOAT'

'A true Olympic and rowing hero, and a story that is both fascinating and truly dramatic'
DAN SNOW, HISTORIAN, OXFORD BLUE

'A remarkable life elegantly, and lovingly, told'
MATT DICKINSON, THE TIMES

'A mesmerising tale of a gilded life set against troubled times. A study of talent and character tested to their limits'
PAUL HAYWARD, CHIEF SPORTS WRITER

'A well-written, rip-roaring rollercoaster read that anyone would enjoy'
BRITISH ROWING

'A fantastic read that will appeal to rowing buffs, biography lovers, and history geeks but also to a wider-audience'
TOM RANSLEY, ROW360

'An exceptional story and a great read, Jamieson's prose is beautiful and makes the history jump off the page'
HENLEY STANDARD

'We modern oarsmen and women are sometimes asked to row as if our lives depended on it: only Jumbo Edwards from the British Olympic rowing family had to do that literally'
SIR MATTHEW PINSENT

'Heartily recommended, to those who enjoy rowing history, good biography, and to those who feast upon good writing'
THOMAS E. WEIL, HEAR THE BOAT SING

Water's Gleaming Gold

The Story of Hugh 'Jumbo' Edwards

Gavin Jamieson

Lapwing

First published in Great Britain in 2023

Reprinted 2024

First edition published in 2023 by
Lapwing Publishing Services
2 Siren Cottages, Horsgate Lane, Cuckfield RH17 5AZ

http://www.lapwingpublishing.com

Copyright © 2023 Gavin Jamieson

Gavin Jamieson has asserted his moral right to be identified as the Author of this work in accordance with the Copyright Designs and Patent Act 1988.

Every effort has been made to trace copyright holders and to obtain their permission for the use of copyright material. The author and publisher apologise for any errors or omissions and would be grateful if notified of any corrections that should be incorporated in future reprints or editions of this book. Any perceived slight of any individual or organisation is purely unintentional.

All rights reserved. Apart from any use permitted under UK copyright law, this publication may not be reproduced, distributed, stored or transmitted in any form or by any means, including photocopying, recording, or other electronic or mechanical methods, without the prior written permission of the publisher or in the case of reprographic production in accordance with the terms of licences issued by the Copyright Licensing Agency.

British Library Cataloguing-in-Publication Data
A catalogue record for this book is available from the British Library

ISBN 978-1-9993226-5-6

Printed and bound by Bell & Bain, Glasgow, UK

Cover design: Tamsin McGee

Front cover: The Great Britain Olympic coxless four of Rowland George, Jack Beresford, Hugh Edwards and John Badcock, Los Angeles, 1932

In remembrance of John and David Edwards

'All through the swing they hear the boat sing'

A Racing Eight (excerpt)

A racing eight of perfect mould,
    True to the builder's law,
That takes the water's gleaming gold
    Without a single flaw.
A ship deep, resonant within,
    Harmonious to the core,
That vibrates to her polished skin
    The tune of wave and oar.

James Lister Cuthbertson (1901)

Contents

	Introduction	vii
	Prologue	xi
1.	Rise of a Dragon	1
2.	Water on the Brain	15
3.	Oxford Blues	23
4.	Prepare to Meet Thy God	27
5.	Leaving Oxford	47
6.	Jumbo Arises	51
7.	Henley Hat-trick	57
8.	Fastest Pair in the World	69
9.	Henley of the Skies	77
10.	The Promised Land	91
11.	Luck of the Moccasins	103
12.	Achieving the Impossible	119
13.	Call me Mike	125
14.	United in Effort	139
15.	Night of the Thousand Bombers	151
16.	Crash Positions	161

17.	Rowing for Survival	175
18.	Return to the Water	181
19.	Dark Blue Redemption	189
20.	The Four Pillars	197
21.	Mutiny on the Isis	201
22.	We Meet Again, Herr Krupp	211
23.	A Farewell to the Water	223
	Epilogue	227
	Acknowledgements	231
	Selected Bibliography	239

Introduction

It was on a blistering hot summer's day when I first encountered the name Jumbo Edwards. It was July 2006 and my first visit to Henley Royal Regatta. Around me in the Stewards' Enclosure were glistening white marquees, flower-decked enclosures and be-flagged boats. Nothing could have been more glorious than this straight 'mile, two furlongs and twenty poles' of the river Thames, like a glittering strip of mirror in the brilliant sunshine. My girlfriend at the time, Melissa, had invited me to the regatta and my surroundings were a world apart from my London office on the polluted and drab Euston Road.

I had no particular interest in rowing. I would watch the Olympic rowing on television every four years, and occasionally the Boat Race. However, my surroundings were beguiling. It was an amalgamation of a sporting crucible, a dainty summer jamboree and an exhibition of British eccentricity. Sitting on one of the green canvassed deckchairs with a Pimms we watched the boats sweep past, their oars striking the water with power and precision.

Queuing up for more refreshments at the bar, I could overhear old men in colourful blazers and caps talking to Melissa. The distinctly comical name 'Jumbo' was excitedly mentioned by those sporting faded Oxford University Boat Club caps. Melissa had told me briefly about her grandfather, Hugh 'Jumbo' Edwards, that he was a well-known Oxford rowing coach and had once competed in the Olympics but he had died just a few months after she was born. Those who talked about Jumbo did so with a passion and recounted memories of a man in a sheepskin jacket barking out instructions on his megaphone to his crew labouring in their boat. Stories were told of a rather reticent man who, with a few words before practice outings, managed to transform oarsmen into dedicated disciples to his cause.

Three years after this day trip to Henley, Melissa and I were married. My father-in-law, David, was the youngest of Jumbo's two sons – John had died in 1983 – and whenever we travelled to Dorset to visit my parents in-law, I would spend hours trawling through the family archive of dusty photograph albums, yellowed correspondence and tarnished rowing medals. It was devastating to find out that the Olympic gold medals, and the British Empire gold medals, had all been stolen a few decades back.

Both David and his older brother John had been talented oarsmen. With his father as coach, David had rowed for Oxford in the Boat Races of 1958 and 1959. The brothers had also won rowing medals for Wales at the Commonwealth Games.

There was talk of a mutiny against his father in 1959, of memories of Jumbo flying bombers in the Second World War and a family that was steeped in the sport of rowing.

Then there was also a bright red ring-binder. This was the unpublished recollections and memoirs that Jumbo had typed out but had been left unfinished. It was entitled *Through the Usual Channels* and dedicated to Alex and Tarquin – his two grandsons. Tarquin, Melissa's brother, had also inherited the Edwards talent for rowing – but a life-changing motorbike accident ended his hopes of following his father and grandfather in gaining a Blue at Oxford.

There was one part of Hugh Edwards life that remained a mystery. He would never talk to his family about his experiences in the RAF during the Second World War. On the typed, but now faded, sheets of paper in the red ring-binder he could not bring himself to recount what happened on a fateful November day when he so narrowly escaped with his life. There was too much loss and sadness. It was only through his wartime logbooks, and years of research, that his heroism could be uncovered.

On those visits to Dorset, David and I would talk long into the evening about the stories of his father. We would read the newspaper stories that my research had uncovered, look through the RAF logbooks and watch old, grainy, silent Pathé news clips of Boat Races from the 1920s. A life less ordinary was emerging. For David, it was important that this extraordinary life of his father was revealed. He asked me to write the memoir of Hugh 'Jumbo' Edwards, to uncover the man behind the myth.

This is his story.

Prologue

Sunday, November 21st, 1943

15.30 hours

Buffeted on the waves of an endless grey expanse of the Atlantic floats a bright yellow inflatable life raft. The English mainland is twelve miles to the east.

There is a solitary bedraggled and sodden figure lying injured and exhausted within the inflatable. Wing Commander Hugh Robert Arthur Edwards struggles to release two flimsy aluminium oars from the onboard supply bags. He begins to row east, fighting against the swell and waves of a wintry Atlantic, leaving behind an expanding patch of oil and the submerging wreckage of his RAF Consolidated B-24 Liberator.

Eleven years previously, on a sweltering Californian day in August 1932, Hugh 'Jumbo' Edwards marched into the cavernous bowl of the Los Angeles Olympic Stadium with his fellow British Olympic team. In front of a closing ceremony crowd of 87,000 spectators, he proudly wore two Olympic gold medals around his neck. Great Britain was celebrating victories in four Olympic events. Two of these – the coxless pair and coxless four in rowing – were won by Edwards and on a single day.

With this extraordinary success, he had finally demonstrated to the rowing world that he was one of the finest oarsman that Britain had produced.

On this late November afternoon – and four days after his thirty-seventh birthday – Hugh Edwards is rowing for his life and darkness is beginning to fall.

Chapter 1

Rise of a Dragon

Westcote Barton is a small village nestling in the West Oxfordshire countryside, with the River Dorn meandering past a collection of cottages. The pretty village church dates to 1086 and was dedicated to St Edmund the Martyr. It was around this church that the cottages of Westcote Barton clustered, and in 1900 a 36-year-old Church of England vicar was appointed to serve the parish.

His name was Reverend Robert Stephen Edwards. Formerly a minor canon at Bangor Cathedral, this was his first appointment as a parish vicar and he brought his young family with him from Wales. His wife, Anne Rosalie Tannatt Pryce, was twenty-eight. The couple had married in Llanfyllin, Montgomeryshire, Wales in 1897 and by the time that they had moved to Oxfordshire they had two infant sons: David, aged two, and Thomas, almost one. The family quickly settled into the vicarage and village life. Two years later, in 1902, their daughter Mary was born.

The family's idyllic life continued until October 1903 when 5-year-old David succumbed to tuberculosis. In the early 20th Century there was no effective treatment to fight this dreaded disease. With the young far more susceptible to the diseases, tuberculosis was called the 'robber of youth'. David was buried in the cemetery of his father's church.

In August 1905, Anne gave birth to another son – Edward Cecil – and although the family struggled to put behind them the sadness of the loss

The vicarage at Westcote Barton, Oxfordshire, where the Edwards family moved to in 1900.

of David, the vicarage was once again bustling with a family of five. Fifteen months later, on November 17th 1906, there was a new addition to the family – Hugh Robert Arthur Edwards was born at home.

Hugh's earliest memories were of playing in the vicarage grounds and in its coalhouses. The young Hugh struck up a keen friendship with the church's sexton, nicknamed 'Brain', who complemented his work with gravedigging, gardening and general handyman duties around the house.

Even at the age of four, Hugh's adventurous spirit would lead him to daring plots. One day, opening the gate at the bottom of the garden, he set off on the road towards the village of Hopcroft's Holt and eventually on to the city of Oxford, already impatient to get on with his life. Fortunately, Hugh only made it as far as the Fox Inn – a short one hundred yard dash from the vicarage – before Brain caught up with the escapee and dragged him back to the house.

Hugh's brother Edward – always referred to as Cecil – was his closest friend after Brain. The two boys were close in age, just over a year separated them, and shared the same sense of adventure. The brothers also shared a French governess and were bi-lingual at a young age. As Hugh stressed when looking back on his childhood, the Edwards family did not have a 'drop of English blood'. 'My father was Welsh, though learned to speak English at school. From school he went to Jesus College, Oxford, before taking Holy Orders. Like all the Welsh he was very musical, with a wonderful voice, and trained the choir of Bangor Cathedral. My mother was half Welsh and half Dutch, a curious mixture. Her maiden name was Pryce and her father, Thomas Pryce, was a landowner and a merchant for John Pryce & Co. of Lombard Street, London and The Hague, trading in tea, coffee and snakeskins. The family had extensive interests in the Dutch East Indies and in Wales they resided at Trederwen Hall, Llansantffraid, Montgomeryshire. My mother's father went out to Batavia, Java, where he had an estate and there met Rosalie Suzanna van Motman, whom he married in 1863. The family left Java and my mother was born in The Hague, Netherlands, but at an early age the family moved to Wales. My parents met at the Pryce's residence at Llanymynech, Montgomeryshire.'

Edwards' parish encompassed three hundred or so worshippers, but he found time to engage in a few hobbies other than his love of music. The children would often hear a cacophony of strange noises and bangs coming from the workshop in the garden.

One morning, Hugh's father proudly pushed a contraption of wheels and levers out of the workshop doors: the family's very own motor car. As Hugh reminisced, 'The car was steam

Hugh, aged eighteen months, taking an early interest in water.

Hugh (left), Cecil (middle) and their father with the motor car contraption, 1909.

driven with a flash boiler and ran very well down the drive to the road. The problem was, as it had not enough power for climbing any gradient, it always had to be towed back by a horse'. This experimental vehicle was eventually replaced by a far more reliable Clement Talbot automobile.

After attempts to provide a mechanised alternative to the family's pony and trap proved unfeasible, the Reverend Edwards looked to the heavens and constructed a planetarium. He built a model of the solar system that consisted of an oil lamp for the sun, the Earth as a white tennis ball, and a ping pong ball representing the moon. By turning a handle the Earth revolved around the sun, and the moon went round the Earth about twelve times as rapidly.

Hugh's father also experimented in the vicarage, much to the alarm of his patient and understanding wife. Having studied and being inspired by the advances in electricity, Reverend Edwards transformed the vicarage into one of the first country houses in Oxfordshire to be fitted with its own electric generating plant. The dynamo was driven by a Ruston-Hornsby oil engine and Hugh's father wired up the house to provide lighting. After many months of electric light, the engine gave out and was returned to the makers for an overhaul. Whilst there for repairs, the firm went bankrupt and the vicarage was once again illuminated by oil lamps and candles.

This life in the vicarage continued until Hugh reached his fifth birthday, in 1911. The children were now at an age when education had to be prioritised. The Reverend Edwards accepted the position of Chaplain New College, Oxford, and the automobile, ponies and trap were all sold. The family moved away from the countryside to 25 St Margaret's Road in the city. Thomas, the eldest son, was enrolled at the local Dragon School. Mona entered the Girls High School and Hugh, along with Cecil, was sent to a nearby nursery school.

'We mostly played with plasticine and sand, but we did begin to learn and write', recalled Hugh.

Much to Hugh's horror his mother soon gave birth to a fourth son. John Oswald Valentine was born on February 14th, 1912, a birthdate that provided inspiration for the addition of his third name. 'I did not fancy having a little brother; he got all the attention, while we had to put up with second best in the form of a nanny.'

One Sunday, Hugh and the recently employed nanny went for a walk along the towpath of the canal. Resplendent in his best white sailor suit but playing too close to the edge of the water, he suddenly fell in with an almighty splash. He quickly managed to scramble out again but was marched home by a panic stricken nanny.

This was to be Hugh's first encounter with the river, and he would make a habit of falling in.

The house in Oxford lacked the freedom and adventure that the vicarage had offered to the children. For Hugh it was unremarkable apart from a few incidents. A chimney fire resulted in the children being entertained with the thrill of the clanging bells of the approaching fire engine, and delighted in the blue-uniformed firemen with their brightly polished brass helmets. Another cherished memory was when the house was due a spring clean and a company, Elliston & Cavell, would arrive with the wonder of a vacuum cleaner. This was a large trailer with a vacuum pump driven by an oil engine stationed in the street outside the house, with long lengths of flexible rubber hose snaking into the house. Hugh's fascination with gadgetry and technological innovations had clearly been inherited from his father.

The Edwards siblings in 1912. Cecil and Mona (back row) with Hugh (front left), Thomas with Oswald sitting on his knee.

The family were not long at the house in St Margaret's Road however when they moved closer to the Dragon School, to a property in Chadlington Road. With a large garden and a bicycle shed, this was much more to Hugh's liking. The garden was dominated by a large, looming oak tree which obstructed light from entering the dining room. Hugh's father, obviously frustrated by his lack of opportunity to experiment in his workshop back in the countryside, decided to blow the tree up with a quantity of gunpowder. This delighted the children but horrified their mother as several very loud, very explosive charges were required to completely rid the garden of the troublesome tree. The neighbours were understandably alarmed.

In January 1913, Hugh – along with his brother Cecil – was enrolled at the Dragon School. It was a happy time for Hugh and Cecil who both adapted quickly to the ethos of the school, especially the sports curriculum.

'The school was just at the end of our road, and the river Cherwell ran past the playing fields about three hundred yards from the school buildings. After two or three lessons from our gym teacher, Purnell, we learnt to swim dangling at the end of a sort of fishing rod with a belt around our waists. There was a small indoor pool where we were tested over four lengths, equivalent to swimming across the Cherwell and back!'

On Hugh's first day his teacher Miss Williams asked the new boys for their names and what they hoped to do when they had grown up. One of Hugh's classmates looked a rather intellectual type, and when Miss

Williams pointed to the 11-year-old she asked, 'And what is your name?' The confident reply came back, 'My name is John Betjeman, and I am going to be a poet'.

Hugh and John struck up a friendship that would last for years, with Dutch ancestry as something that they both had in common. Also amongst Hugh's classmates was Hugh Gaitskell, but at that age he had not yet developed the confidence to predict that he would be the future leader of the Labour party.

Tragically, the happiness of the family was to be shattered once more. On July 17th, 1914, Hugh's eldest brother Thomas died from meningitis at the age of fourteen.

The family returned to Oxfordshire for the funeral. Robert once again had the desperately sad task of burying a son. Thomas was laid to rest alongside his brother David in the churchyard of Westcote Barton.

School provided a distraction from the sadness at home, and it was at school where lifelong friends were made. That same year also witnessed the advent of the First World War.

Hugh recalls watching as trenches were dug in the local park. It was thrilling for Hugh to look on as trainee soldiers charged at sandbags with fixed bayonets. At the Dragon school, as war raged across the Channel, the boys constructed a lengthy escape tunnel in the playing fields.

Back at the house, Cecil and Hugh built toy submarines, cannons and bombs. Depth charges were devised from gramophone-needle tins, filled with gunpowder and a fuse, bound with iron wire and finally dipped in paraffin wax to make them watertight. The boys would then proceed to a quiet spot by the river and attempt to sink the toy boats that they had built to recreate the daring missions of the British Navy.

During the Summer months the family would holiday in West Wittering, on the South Coast, and the war remained far away. They had friends who had lost sons in the conflict but, as a family, life continued. All four of the children were enjoying school and Hugh's father settled into his role as Chaplain.

Then shattering news arrived in April 1918. The family received a telegram that Hugh's uncle, Thomas Pryce, Anne's brother, had been killed in action during the German Spring Offensive.

The German Spring Offensive was Germany's last attempt to defeat the British and French armies on the Western Front, and thereby win total victory. The revolution in Russia had freed up German units in the east and they had a brief window of opportunity to win a decisive victory before the arrival into the war of overwhelming American forces. Between March 21st and April 30th, 1918, the British lost 236,000 men. Estimated German losses were 348,000. It was into this maelstrom of bullets and shells that Thomas Pryce would make his last stand.

Thomas had been born in the Hague, Netherlands, fifteen years after Hugh's mother. As such, Anne and her eldest sister, Mary, took close care of their infant brother Thomas when the Pryce family moved back to Wales from the Continent. Anne remained very close to 'Tommy', and with the age difference it was as much a maternal love as a sibling one. The news of his death was devastating for her.

Shortly after the outbreak of the First World War, Thomas had enlisted in the Honourable Artillery Company as a private. After a month with his unit in France he had already been promoted to the rank of Lance Corporal. On receiving his commission, he transferred to the 1/6th Battalion, Gloucestershire Regiment, then serving on the Western Front as part of the 48th Division. In late November 1915, after heavy fighting in the village of Gommecourt – sixteen miles south of Arras – Thomas was awarded the Military Cross for leading an assault on German trenches. The initial attack was successful but when German reinforcements arrived, Thomas ensured a safe retreat of the men. During this rapid withdrawal, Thomas was seriously wounded and he was evacuated back to England for treatment.

Thomas was keen to get back to his battalion and a return to the frontline. In May 1916 he once again displayed immense bravery in the face of a German offensive. Thomas was awarded a bar to his MC for leading a platoon in an attack at Fauquissart – forty miles north of his heroics at the village of Gommecourt.

Four months later, in September 1916, Thomas transferred to the 4th Battalion of the Grenadier Guards and was promoted to Lieutenant. He was mentioned in despatches on April 7th 1918 for his services in the field and three days later was promoted to Acting Captain. Within three and a half years, Thomas had risen to the rank of Captain, received a bar to his MC, and been involved in several frontline offensives. This would have been an eventful war for any soldier on the Western Front but, three short days after his promotion, Thomas was to face the fearsome German Spring Offensive.

Thomas's battalion, as part of the 31st Division, had been in reserve but was brought back to the frontline on April 10th to hold the line at the small town of Le Paradis – nineteen miles to the west of Lille. As Captain of a company, he was tasked with the capture and subsequent defence of a nearby village.

> 'Having been ordered to attack a village he personally led forward two platoons, working from house to house, killing some thirty of the enemy, seven of whom he killed himself. The next day he was occupying a position with some thirty to forty men, the remainder of his company having become casualties. As early as 08.15 hours, his left flank was surrounded and the enemy was enfilading him. He was attacked no less than four times during the day, and each time beat off the hostile attack, killing many of the enemy. Meanwhile the enemy brought three field guns to within 300 yards of his line, and were firing over open sights and knocking his trench in. At 18.15 hours, the enemy had worked to within sixty yards of his trench. He then called on his men, telling them to cheer and charge the enemy and fight to the last. Led by Captain Pryce, they left their trench and drove back the enemy with the bayonet some 100 yards. Half an hour later the enemy had again approached in stronger force. By this time Captain Pryce had only 17 men left, and every round of his ammunition had been fired. Determined that there should be no surrender, he once again led his men forward in a bayonet charge, and was last seen engaged in a fierce

hand-to-hand struggle with overwhelming numbers of the enemy. With some forty men he had held back at least one enemy battalion for over ten hours. His company undoubtedly stopped the advance through the British line, and thus had great influence on the battle' *(London Gazette, May 21st, 1918)*

His body was never found. Thomas left behind a wife, Margaret, and three daughters, the cousins of Hugh.

On April 12th, 1919, King George V presented the Victoria Cross to Margaret at a ceremony at Buckingham Palace. His Army Commander later wrote to his widow: 'There is no finer stand in the history of the British Army than this to which Captain Pryce contributed very largely.'

For Hugh, the bravery of his Uncle Tommy was to have a profound effect on his life.

Shortly after the presentation of the Victoria Cross at Buckingham Palace, the family were on the move. Once again, the impetus for this move was the schooling of the children.

Both Hugh and Cecil had left Dragon and were accepted at Westminster School, to commence in September 1919. A friend of Hugh's at Dragon recalled the entry exam for acceptance at Westminster. 'One of the questions asked was "Give a brief sketch of Charles I". Hugh kept it brief and did a drawing of a middle-aged monarch complete with beard.'

Despite this – or perhaps because of this – he was accepted along with Cecil and so the family moved to London and to a house in Addison Gardens, near Shepherd's Bush. Hugh's sister, Mona, was sent to board at Cheltenham Ladies College, and the boys were kitted out in their new school uniform.

'Our school uniform at Westminster was (except when you were a very small boy) a morning coat, spongebag trousers, top hat and cane or tightly rolled umbrella. We wore a jampot collar, with little clips to hold the tie down in place. Only if you got your 'pink' or became a monitor were you permitted to wear a butterfly collar. Black ties were *de rigueur*.'

For the two brothers it was a forty-minute journey into school. 'We went daily by Inner Circle underground from High Street Kensington, with a twenty-minute walk to the station. Children would regularly jeer and shout "Top 'ats" at us.'

Hugh would have started school every morning with a short service in the Poet's Corner of Westminster Abbey. The evening finished with Latin prayers before going home. There were five 'houses', of which College was reserved for King's scholars, and the boys were assigned to Ashburnham.

As at Dragon School, sport was a subject that appealed greatly to both Hugh and Cecil. Their father had rowed for Jesus College when he was studying at Oxford, and was enthusiastic for the boys to also venture out onto the water. 'My father always had an ambition that his sons should get Blues so, when I went to Westminster, I naturally elected for the water in preference to cricket or football.'

At that time, in 1919, Westminster had no boathouse, but used the facilities further down the Thames at London Rowing Club. Throughout Hugh's first term – and at the age of thirteen – he never went out on the river at all but was confined to using the 'tank'. This water-filled training device contained a single seat in which Hugh was taught to perfect the movements of the body by combining the muscle groups and to move the blade of the oar accurately through the water.

Finally, Hugh was allowed on to the river. He was to fall instantly in love with being on the water. Hugh was provided with a 'rum-tum' – a clinker-built racing-boat for one, with outriggers and a sliding seat. The bow and stern were decked in so that it would not swamp in the choppy waters of the Thames, commonplace when the wind and current were moving in opposite directions. This boat was supplied to the school from Bowers & Phelps, the boatbuilders located next to London Rowing Club. Bowers & Phelps was run by the famed boat builder and the King's Bargemaster, John Thomas Phelps, better known as 'Bossie' Phelps. Hugh could not have known at the time that his first encounter with Bossie was to be the start of a long friendship between the two.

Both brothers embraced the art and techniques of single sculling along the Thames, and for Hugh it would have an impact on his academic studies. 'I did not rise to any great heights of brilliance; rather the contrary. On one occasion the remarks from my form master in my school report read, "Progressing slowly, but backwards".'

Despite the promise he was showing on the water, Hugh was always aware of the danger of failing in his studies and being asked to leave the school.

'It was always a hard struggle to avoid getting the "chop". We learnt just a smattering of science on the classical side and I enjoyed that. I also enjoyed the art classes, where we would usually be told to go out into the cloisters or Abbey and draw anything of one's choice. One sometimes got an opportunity to explore the lesser-known parts of the Abbey, and climbing the steps inside the flying buttresses up to the triforium, and onto the roof of King Henry VII's chapel.'

When the family moved to London they invested in a new car: a Model T Ford. With the children all at home for Easter in 1920, Hugh's parents decided to take the family and car across the Channel and spend the holidays in France.

'We had to pack in six of us and our luggage into the car, and it was quite an achievement and no doubt quite a sight to see us packed in and the luggage strapped to the running boards.'

Although Hugh's parents saw this trip as an opportunity to provide the children with a chance to practise their French and to experience life outside of England, the main reason was to visit Flanders. Hugh's mother was desperate to search for any sign of a headstone engraved with the name of her brother, Thomas Pryce.

Hugh found their journey into Flanders a chastening one. For a boy of fourteen years, the excitement of war was about to be doused with a grim reality.

'The roads were in very bad condition, the pot holes could not be avoided and the speed was reduced to a snail's pace. It was very depressing on the Western Front; villages in rubble, trees in splinters, barbed wire everywhere. The trenches were still there, and the occasional pill boxes, and one didn't have to walk far before finding rifles, bayonets, ammunition and unexploded grenades. It was difficult to imagine how men could have lived in the trenches and dugouts.'

The family were aware that Tommy was last seen in a location near to the village of Le Paradis. When they reached Le Paradis there was nothing but rubble. The village had all but been destroyed. It was a vast difference from any paradise that the name implied.

Anne searched the names in the nearby graveyards of British soldiers, with a desperate hope to find the resting place of her brother. Sadly, the reports were true. The body of Tommy was never found.

Chapter 2

Water on the Brain

Hugh Edwards continued to struggle with his academic studies at Westminster – but was excelling on the water.

The origins of rowing as an amateur sport are debated widely amongst historians. As with the advent of so many rulebooks and clubs, the sport of rowing can be traced back to the public schools of England. In the book *Boating* by W. B. Woodgate, published in 1888, a chapter on rowing at Eton College is included and rowing seems to have been among the amusements of Etonians at least as early as the middle of the 18th Century.

Westminster School's claim to having organised rowing for the boys dates back to 1813 and an entry in the *Water Ledger* with the names of six boys who rowed in a boat called *The Fly*.

While Eton and Westminster were apparently the two earliest schools at which rowing was undertaken, at neither was it a competitive sport. Westminster did not have its first recorded race until some years later. At Eton, rowing took the form of a leisurely paddle to a meadow downstream where refreshments were partaken, before rowing back to Windsor. Neither was rowing at Eton or Westminster the first expression of recreational rowing. It was practised elsewhere well before it appeared at either school. However, in the 18th Century, it would have been the former students from both Eton and Westminster who were among the leading advocates at Cambridge and Oxford to introduce intramural rowing competitions among the various colleges on both campuses, eventually giving rise to rowing as a sport.

Whereas Westminster had a long and fascinating history of rowing, the sport had ceased to be on the curriculum for the boys in 1884. Rowing was not re-commenced until 1914, five years before Hugh and Cecil were enrolled as students.

Although rowing had been mothballed for over thirty years, the headmaster James Gow had reinstated it and – with hopes of Westminster once again becoming competitive – the school employed a number of coaches. M. H. Ellis, who had rowed for Oxford in the Boat Race of 1920 and 1921, joined the staff. Ellis was joined by M. Watkins, who had rowed at Cambridge, and J. G. Jeffries from Geelong School in Melbourne, Australia.

As well as single sculling, Hugh was competing for Westminster in their eight, and in the four for his house. In 1923, at the age of sixteen, Hugh was entered in the Gilowen Sculls Challenge Trophy – an annual event on the Thames. The appeal to Hugh was not only the trophy itself, but that the winner was presented with a gold shield engraved with the school coat of arms for your watch chain. Hugh's father asked him what his chances were of winning.

'I replied that I thought I had a reasonably good chance, and though my steering was poor, I should feel certain of success if only I had a "seebackroscope". This was an optical instrument worn in the eye like a monocle, and enabled you to see backwards. My father said he would go to Gamages (a local store) and buy one, and meet at Putney in time for the race. Arriving at Putney I met him and he told me he had been to Gamages and seen the "seebackroscope" and that they were rubbishy things and not worth having. He could invent something better. I was terribly disappointed, but knowing the river as we boys did, I nevertheless managed to avoid running into the riverbank and won the trophy.'

Hugh and his classmates were always enthralled by the annual Boat Race between Oxford and Cambridge. Times achieved in practice were published on an almost daily basis in the newspapers, and the boys took an intense interest.

Hugh's infatuation enraged his form master, A. T. Willett, who frustratingly declared that 'he had water on the brain'. He had to study his books and not the river.

The Boat Race has been a key event in the British sporting calendar since it was first established in 1829. Like the Grand National and the FA Cup Final, the Boat Race was – and remains – a spectacle that almost everyone in the country would take some form of interest in, regardless of their feeling for the sport. In the 1940s the journalist Louis T. Stanley remarked that the race was 'unique, the only occasion in this country of a highly specialised sport commanding an unprecedented public appeal', one at which 'spectators to whom Oxford and Cambridge could be but vague names sported Dark and Light Blue favours'.

Victory or defeat, however fractional, was always how a crew was to be remembered.

For Hugh, the Boat Race was the highlight of his year. 'We devoured the daily press reports on the progress of the crews, there was not a thing we didn't know about them and their famous coaches, usually F. J. Escombe for Cambridge and Harcourt Gilbey Gold for Oxford. For us, the crews of 1923 and 1924 were giants on the earth in those days: P. C. Mallam, who later coached many Oxford crews, G. O. ("Gully") Nickalls one of the classic oars, A. C. Irvine who later fell off the top of Mount Everest, C. R. M. Eley and J. A. Macnabb of Cambridge who were Olympic Gold medal winners.'

As Hugh recalled, Andrew 'Sandy' Irvine was in the losing Oxford crew for the Boat Race in 1922 and a member of the winning crew in 1923 – as it would turn out the only time in twenty-two years that Oxford would win between 1914 and 1936. However, Irvine's passion for rowing was only exceeded by his love for the mountains. At Oxford, he joined the

Westminster School boys jostling for the best positions to watch the Boat Race.

Oxford University Mountaineering Club and took part in the Merton College Arctic Expedition to Spitsbergen, Norway, where he excelled on every front. In 1923, the expedition's leader, Noel Odell, invited Irvine to join the forthcoming third British Mount Everest expedition on the grounds that he might be the 'superman' that the expedition felt it needed. Irvine was at the time a 21-year-old undergraduate student.

While attempting the first successful ascent of Mount Everest, Irvine and his climbing partner George Mallory disappeared somewhere high on the mountain's fearsome northeast ridge. The pair were last sighted only a few hundred metres from the summit. It remains a highly debated mystery as to whether the pair reached the summit before they perished. Mallory's body was found in 1999, but Irvine's body and portable camera have never been found.

Cecil, Hugh's brother, was also excelling at rowing and was appraised – even by Hugh – as the superior talent. For three years, 1923 to 1925, Hugh rowed in the first eight at Westminster and for the first two of those years alongside Cecil. In 1924, Cecil was elected the 'Head of Water' (captain of rowing in 'Westminster-speak') and as such was invited to write his report on the state of rowing in the school.

> 'I think we may now fairly claim that Westminster is a first-class rowing school again. The eight this year was inferior only to Shrewsbury among the schools, and they were probably the best eight at Henley. Mr Harcourt Gold said he wished Eton would row again in the style in which we rowed this year; he could pay us no higher compliment. But we have had no rowing Blue from Westminster for over forty years, and unfortunately we have not yet won a heat at Henley regatta. If only the school would realise that Westminster is (as in the first half of last century) in the very first rank of rowing schools, and that the school's reputation depends on rowing; whereas in cricket and football it holds no such position and has no such traditions, I feel sure that a larger percentage of the school would help to maintain our prestige. Westminster has the disadvantage that it is distant from the part of the river where it can practise – but rowing is the most noble sport in the world and Westminster should be one of the chief nurseries of the art in the country.'

The award of a 'Blue' is the highest sporting honour granted to individual students at Oxford and Cambridge. Cecil was not aware then that within twelve months he would have the opportunity to end the long, barren record of those forty years and to win a rowing Blue at Oxford. By doing so he would be restoring a pride in rowing for Westminster School.

At this point, Hugh had become so keen on the water that after the outings in the eight he would spend a considerable amount of time by himself sculling – and one of his rowing heroes was Jack Beresford Junior.

Even though there was no Jack Beresford Senior, Jack was widely referred to as 'Beresford Jr' and his father Julius was known as 'Beresford Sr'. Jack had inherited his father's talent for rowing, and so the addition of 'Junior' was merely to differentiate the two in the newspapers of the time. Rowing in the coxed four at the 1912 Olympic Games, Julius Beresford had won a silver medal for Great Britain.

Young Jack was establishing himself as one of the most talented scullers that Britain had produced. In 1920 Beresford won the Diamond Challenge Sculls – the single sculls event at Henley – and followed this up with a silver medal at the 1920 Olympic Games in Antwerp. Also in that year he won for the first time the Wingfield Sculls, the British Amateur Sculling Championship of the Thames. Jack would go on to win this competition for an astonishing seven consecutive years, a streak unmatched in history.

For Hugh, this made Jack a giant amongst men. He was far too shy to approach Jack to talk to him about rowing – but he had another ploy.

As Hugh would later admit, 'I sometimes used to lie in wait near Hammersmith for Jack Beresford and scull back to Putney trying to keep my distance of four lengths ahead of him. This exercise helped me immeasurably and I became quite fast.'

As Cecil mentioned in his address to the School in 1924, Westminster's crew had grown in strength and ability. They were now competing at the world's most prestigious rowing regatta, Henley Royal Regatta.

In 1923, with both Hugh and Cecil in the boat, the Westminster eight were selected to compete in the Ladies' Challenge Plate at Henley. Back then the Ladies' Challenge Plate was originally for British academic institutions and Trinity College Dublin.

The lack of any competitive first-class racing experience was certainly apparent with the Westminster eight – they were defeated in the first round, losing by eleven lengths to a dominant Magdalen College. The Field admirably summed up their racing capabilities when it reported, 'They plugged away, and were tired. But, though a crew must be judged primarily on its racing, it is at the same time encouraging to be able to say that the Eight was rowing in the right way. They had an easy, natural swing, and a quick grip of the water behind the rigger.'

The Elizabethan – the Westminster School magazine originally started by pupils in 1874 – gave a verdict on the performance of the brothers:

> Stroke (E. C. T. EDWARDS). As a stroke he gave his crew a certain amount of length and rhythm, but he was unable to keep them going at a fast stroke. He is a hard worker, and will improve if he can get out of the habit of pushing away his slide at the beginning of the stroke, and tearing out the finish with his arms.
>
> Number 6 (H. R. A. EDWARDS). Developed into one of the most promising members of the crew. He has a natural style, and now that he has learnt to control his slide, he should be very useful next year.

The following year the Westminster crew performed better but again were eliminated. This time they lost by a length and a half to a fast Pembroke College crew which contained two Blues and had been second on the river at Cambridge. It was a fine achievement for eight schoolboys who were going up against a far more experienced crew.

Hugh was philosophical about their performance.

'Although we failed at Henley against college crews like Pembroke, I do not think we need have failed. If, in the few days practice we had before Henley we could have had a few short trial rows against College and Grand crews and been brought to realise that we were not so inferior, I think we could better have acquitted ourselves.'

This determination and self-belief were to serve Hugh well in the years to come.

Hugh's first experiences of Henley had lit a flame – a desire to be the best, to win.

Chapter 3

Oxford Blues

In July 1924, Cecil left Westminster School and went up to Christ Church, Oxford. He soon embraced the rowing culture at Christ Church and his talent was such that he was selected for the 1925 eight to compete at the Boat Race. Hugh's pride in his older brother was immeasurable. Cecil had become one of the giants that the Westminster boys idolised.

Cecil had also fulfilled the prophecy that he made as Head of the Water: in 1925 he became Westminster's first Blue in over forty years.

The Oxford crew that Cecil rowed in was dogged by sickness throughout practice and five days before the race the bow – D. C. Bennett – fell ill and had to be replaced by the spare man, A. H. Franklin.

On Saturday March 28th, 1925, the day of the race, a fresh north westerly wind was blowing. It was soon apparent that the conditions on the Thames were going to be challenging.

The Edwards family had joined the tens of thousands that were lining the banks to cheer on the crews. Hugh had jostled himself into the throng of supporters by the riverside in Putney so that he could cheer on his brother at the start – but he was acutely aware that the crew who lost the toss would inevitably have to row in the very choppy water of the Surrey Station. To Hugh's despair, Cambridge won the toss.

The Oxford crew for the Boat Race, 1925. Cecil is third from left.

The Press reported on the drama of that stormy day.

'There was tremendous excitement at the start. The crowds were larger than ever, mighty cheers went up for both boats as they embarked. Oxford, "challenging the river", went out first. Five minutes later the Cambridge boat took the water, and the cox sent it almost directly over to the sheltered Middlesex side. They had won the toss, and all the watermen declared that the race was already lost and won. Tradition has it that the Surrey side is the winning side, but not when crested waves have turned the river into a sea. So rough was the water that it was difficult to get the boats to their starting positions. A hundred thousand eyes were focussed on the crews. The starting flag went down. The Oxford oars dipped quickly into the water, and they were away. Cambridge were slower with the start, but steadiness was essential in the rough waters. Though the Oxford stroke pulled away at thirty-two strokes to the minute, compared to the Cambridge thirty-one, they only secured a short lead for a short distance. The waves bore on them, and acted like four-wheel brakes on a motor car. Cambridge were content to hold their own in the calm wall-protected water. Within minutes the

Dark Blues were struggling in rough water, Cambridge were rowing in a river. Small wonder that the Light Blues went ahead. Small wonder that the space between the two boats opened out wider and wider until the race had become a procession. And then disaster. Opposite Harrods the Oxford boat seemed to be sinking. It went deeper and deeper into the water, and not all the proud physique of eight trained men could pull it at a racing pace. After a mile things became worse. The boat was deep in the water and still it shipped more. The Oxford boat approached Hammersmith and the gunwales became submerged. It looked as though the boat would surely sink. The cox was sitting in water, the oarsmen were paddling in, yet they rowed on. Far ahead, the Cambridge boat rode lightly on the calmer reach above the bridge. With laboured strokes the Oxford boat passed beneath the bridge, and soon afterwards the coach instructed them to pull for the shore. They did so, but refused to recognise defeat. Quite close to the Surrey side they crossed, and then rowed while indescribable agony was depicted on all their faces. Eventually their boat sank beneath them, and they stopped in abject misery. Meanwhile the Cambridge boat, travelling well, disappeared toward Mortlake. The Light Blues rowed as though still challenged until Chiswick Bridge was reached, and then, in the final reach, they paddled home to victory.' (*Press and Journal, March 30th, 1925*)

Cecil was devastated. With the disruption to the crew and losing the all-important toss, Oxford's defeat was not a surprise.

Cecil hid his disappointment well. When interviewed by the Press, he maintained a steady, inscrutable expression. One of the newspapers described him as possessing the mysterious gaze of the Sphinx. From that moment on he would be known affectionately to one and all as 'Sphinx'.

For A. H. Franklin – the late replacement at bow – he became the only Blue who had never completed a row down the four-mile course from Putney to Mortlake, either in practice or in the race. Cecil tried to comfort him, but throughout the evening while the rest of the crew were drowning their sorrows in London's West End, he was morose at the

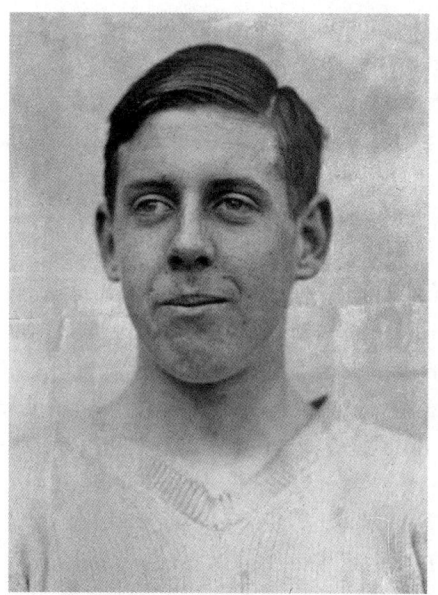

Cecil Edwards, aged twenty, photographed before the Boat Race in 1926.

thought that he had not justified the award of his Blue. Franklin went to bed early and next morning went down to Putney and borrowed a sculling boat.

Those walking along the banks on their early commute watched as a solitary figure rowed from Putney down to the finish line at Mortlake. As Cecil reported to Hugh later that day, 'At last Franklin could smile again'.

All the excitement and drama of the day only increased Hugh's absolute determination to earn his Blue and row in the Boat Race.

As he stood on the bank with the throngs of cheering spectators, watching his brother powering the Oxford boat through the choppy waters, he was not to know that in just one year he would be in that boat.

If the Boat Race of 1925 was described as 'eventful', the following year's Boat Race would surpass the drama.

At the centre of this rowing drama would be one oarsman: the 19-year-old Hugh Edwards.

Chapter 4

Prepare to Meet Thy God

Hugh was desperate to follow his older brother Cecil to Oxford. This desire was matched with choosing the College that he believed would be best able to fulfil his insatiable need to row. There were only three Oxford colleges worth his consideration: Christ Church, Magdalen and New College. Hugh was delighted when a letter of acceptance from Christ Church arrived at his parental home. He would be joining his brother.

Starting his studies at Christ Church in October 1925, Hugh immediately signed up for rowing.

In a photographic portrait of Hugh – taken at Gillman & Co. Studios shortly after he arrived in Oxford – a confident man stares back into the lens. His brown hair is neatly combed to one side, revealing a narrow strip of white skin on a prominent forehead. This whiteness differentiated from a tanned complexion, gained from rowing in the Summer months. His thin lips are pursed but he still retains a look of amusement. A month short of his nineteenth birthday, Hugh had grown into a handsome fellow, ready to take on the world.

The years he had dedicated to rowing on the Thames with Westminster was in evidence to the coaches. Standing at just under six foot tall, and with a muscular body that had been developed by pacing against the great Jack Beresford, he was in perfect shape.

In that first term, Hugh was selected to row in the first four.

A year previously, in 1924, Christ Church had a winning eight at the Head of the River but narrowly lost the prestigious Grand Challenge Cup at Henley Royal Regatta, beaten by Leander. Of this highly lauded crew, five remained, and the College decided to enter two crews for the University fours.

Much to his personal embarrassment, due to his inexperience, Hugh was selected for the first four. 'As a freshman, I felt that I had not yet proved my worth to those older than myself. I knew I was fast in the boat but many saw me as inexperienced and so I had to practise harder and longer than all the others.'

Hugh Edwards, aged eighteen, photographed at Gillman & Co. Studios, Oxford, 1925.

Along with Hugh, the four consisted of Peter Murray-Threipland and two Blues who rowed in the previous year's ill-fated Boat Race: Chris Pitman and Hugh's brother Cecil.

The faith that the coaches showed in the 19-year-old Hugh was justified, his crew won the University fours.

This victory in his first term, along with a win in the Silver Sculls, resulted in the Oxford coach – Dr Gilbert 'Beja' Bourne – selecting Hugh for the 1926 Varsity crew and the Boat Race. At the age of nineteen, he would be realising his lifelong dream.

Hugh was described by his fellow rower Chris Pitman as 'young for his years, shy and reserved'. By Hugh's own admission, he was also rather conceited. His initial feeling as an inexperienced 'interloper' had been

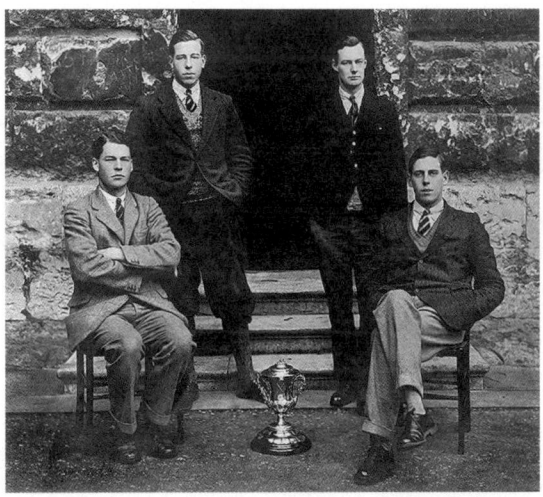

The Christ Church crew after victory in the Oxford University coxless fours, 1925. Back row (left-to-right): Hugh, Chris Pitman. Front row (left-to-right): Peter Murray-Threipland, Cecil. All four would be selected for the Boat Race in 1926.

superseded. This conceit was fed by the success he had already achieved in his first term and his selection for the Varsity crew.

The self-confidence was countered by the overall feeling that 'being an Oxford crew we couldn't possibly win'. This pessimism of Hugh's enveloped all of Oxford, a consequence of the dismal results since the resumption of the Boat Race on the Thames after the First World War.

Since 1920, Oxford had only been victorious once – in 1923 – and then by only three-quarters of a length. This losing mentality had a detrimental effect on the training programme that was about to begin for Hugh early in January 1926.

In his unpublished recollections, Hugh describes the Oxford crew for the 1926 Boat Race.

'The crew that was finally formed for the race in 1926 consisted of Peter Murray-Threipland at bow. Tim Shaw, at two, had been in the Shrews-

The Oxford eight for the Boat Race, 1926. Back row (left-to-right): P. W. Murray-Threipland, T. W. Shaw, G. H. Crawford, Hugh, Cecil, C. E. Pitman. Front row: W. Rathbone, J. D. W. Thomson.

bury crew which won the Ladies' Plate at Henley in 1924. Geoffrey Crawford was at three, like all Brasenose men of the time he was a great character and always kept the crew in good spirits. William 'Nono' Rathbone was at number four. He was a Radley Boy, and a tower of strength though perhaps a bit rough. I was at five, and James 'Spud' Thomson was at six. My brother Cecil 'Sphinx' Edwards was at seven and Chris Pitman stroke. Sir James Croft was cox.'

Each academic year at Oxford University is divided into three terms: Michaelmas term from October to December; Hilary term from January to March; and Trinity term from April to June. In Michaelmas, the crew was coached in the morning in 'tub pairs'. A 'tub pair' was a wooden training boat fitted out for two crew – with the coach sitting in the stern and barking out orders. The purpose of this was to iron out faults and improve oarmanship before the crew got settled in the actual boat. In the afternoons, the crew would go out in the eight with the coach on the towpath keeping up alongside on his bicycle.

By the time that Hilary term started in the New Year – and after about two weeks training - the crew were beginning to settle down. The Proctors of the Colleges would forbid any rowing in the mornings in term time and so the morning tub pairs ceased. At the end of a further two weeks of training the President informed the crew to order their kit. This included a white sweater trimmed with blue ribbon – with the initials of the rower embroidered across the chest – blue 'stockings', blanket trousers, blue blazer, blue dinner jacket and trimmed white waistcoat to match with white trousers for evening wear. As Hugh fondly recalled, once the kit arrived he felt enormous pride and that this truly was the realisation of his dream.

From the fifth week, the crew was moved into 'strict training'. Hugh could always recite the mantra: 'No smoking, no cinemas, 7.30 a.m. training run, 10.30 p.m. bed'.

Additionally, each oarsman in turn would provide breakfast for the others in their rooms. Fulfilling a long Oxford tradition, a crew member would also provide a bunch of violets for their buttonholes which were to be obtained from an early visit to the flower market.

In the seventh week of training, even though the academic term had yet to finish, the crew moved down river to a long reach of water at Bourne End and took up residence at the Spade Oak Ferry Hotel. The boat was housed in the boathouse of Rudolph Lehmann. 'Rudy' was a legendary Oxford rowing coach and between the years 1877 and 1888 he had the notable distinction of finishing last in every heat he entered at the Henley Regatta.

At the end of the eighth week, the crew moved down to Putney and this is when the training became a lot more varied and interesting:

'In truth, training up until now had been infinitely dreary, slogging up and down the river with no aim or object in sight, and the Boat Race itself hidden away in the womb of the future. We never had another crew alongside us for pacing; we never knew how fast or how slowly we were going. We had to endure a cutting east wind, insufficiently clad with bare knees. Frequently splashes of water would freeze immediately on the oar handles. Tucked away in the wastes of Bourne, we did not even have an audience to perform for except for the visits of the Press Correspondents who seldom said anything nice. It was not a joyous time.'

Hugh's core belief was that for a crew to go fast, they must have an '*esprit de corps*'. It was imperative that they all get on well together ashore as well as being uniform on the water. They must all think alike. There must be no discrimination, unconscious or conscious. This is how you get the boat to fly, to sing, in the water. This is how you beat Cambridge.

In the Oxford crew there were a number of like-minded men. There were five who had rowed together in the excellent Christ Church Head of the River crew (including Sphinx) and three Etonians, but Hugh was the only freshman. After two months of intensive training, the eight were beginning to form that trust in one another that was so crucial. To strengthen that *esprit de corps* the crew were put up in a house on Putney Hill, about a mile away from their headquarters at London Rowing Club.

For the next four weeks, up to the date of the Boat Race, the crew in Hugh's words, 'were subjected to a continuous barrage of publicity'.

For those in the crew who had not experienced the Boat Race, the first outing to Putney was frightening. It was recalled by Hugh that, 'taking the boat out one had to run the gauntlet, not only of the general public, not only of the press photographers, but also the cine-cameras of Pathé and Gaumont'.

Such was the clamour and interest by the public in the Boat Race that there were articles published in the newspapers on a daily basis concerning the form of the crews. The Oxford crew were so besieged by autograph hunters that the cox, Sir James Croft, took it upon himself to forge the signatures of his crew to relieve them of this time-consuming chore. Cartoonists for the periodicals, such as *The Tatler* and *The Sketch*, were constantly amongst the crew on the bank and by the boathouse. The crew's only sanctuary away from this intrusion was in the house on Putney Hill.

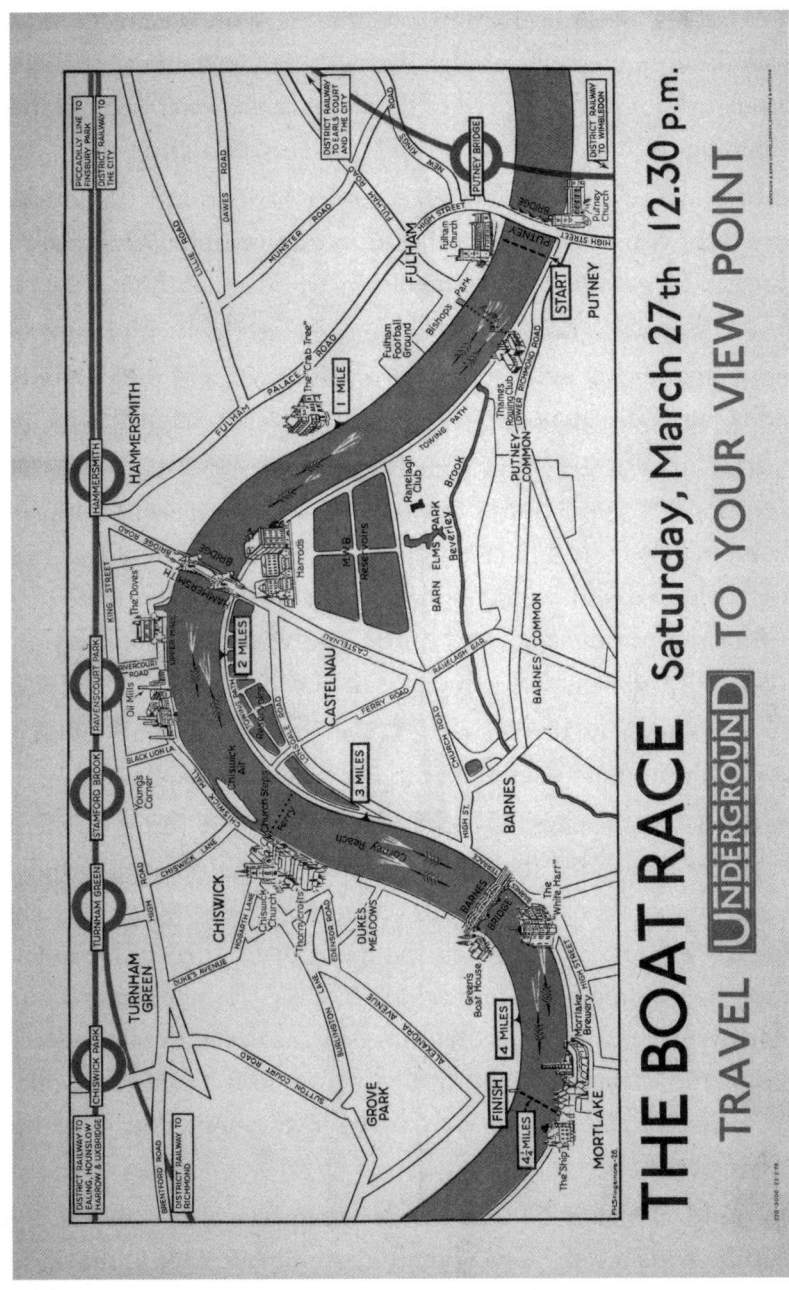

The London Transport Poster for the Boat Race, 1926, detailing the course and the viewing points © TfL from the London Transport Museum collection.

These last few weeks before the day of the race were used by the coaches to work the crew up to what Hugh described as a 'racing pitch'. This term encapsulated not just the speed of the boat on the water, but the morale and fighting spirit of the crew.

Herbert Hartley, who a few years earlier had stroked Cambridge to victory three years running, was heard to exclaim about Oxford: 'I hate the bugger. I regard them as Germans'.

These words were used as further incentive to the Oxford crew when facing scratch eights during practice on the river, and these opponents would be easily dispatched.

A useful ally was gained in famed boat builder and the King's Bargemaster, Bossie Phelps. Bossie was one of the watermen of Putney and knew intimately every stretch and bend on the 4.2 miles of the Thames course. Twice a day he would sit down with Sir James Croft and go over with him the intricacies of the course and where every advantage, no matter how small, could be gained for the Oxford boat.

The weeks and days quickly passed in a routine of practice, more practice, and for Sir James the task of forging more autographs.

The day before the race, the crew had only one short outing on the river. The coaches demanded that the crew row at 'high pressure' – building to thirty-four strokes at the end of one minute, after which they all felt completely exhausted. For Hugh the thought occurred to him that the next day he would have to row at high intensity for not just one minute but for twenty, and in front of an immense expectant crowd exceeding 250,000. The thought of this, 'turned my muscles to jelly'. He put this down to nerves and had an early night in the hope that sleep would quickly descend.

On Saturday, March 27th, the crew woke up to a gloriously fine morning with a gentle breeze blowing south to south-east. Due to the tide conditions, that year's Boat Race was to start at an earlier time of 12.30 p.m. By 8 a.m. large numbers of crowds were already making their way to the banks of the Thames to ensure they had secured the best vantage points to see the crews speed past. One hour later, barges and tugs began to fuss about the starting point to make sure everything was in order. There was plenty of activity along the towpath, with a large police force beginning to handle the growing crowds. Numerous 'hawkers' set up stalls selling food, drink, rosettes and other trinkets to allow the spectators to proudly display which crew they were cheering for.

Opinions as to the prospects of the rivals seemed to be evenly divided amongst the newspapers and correspondents. However, the apparent exhaustion of the Oxford crew during the short practice of the previous day had not gone unnoticed and this led to a slight favouring for the Light Blues of Cambridge. Bossie Phelps was reluctant to speak to the press but when they managed to get him to utter a few words during the morning he simply declared, 'In fact, I think there will be very little in it'.

The French polishers had spent the greater part of the night giving the finishing touches to the Oxford boat, ensuring that it was in the best possible condition to take to the water. Shortly after 9 a.m., the Oxford crew arrived on the scene for a brief row. As the *Yorkshire Evening Post* correspondent reported, 'they all looked bronzed and fit'.

At 10 a.m., the sun broke through the mist hanging over the river. It was a little under three hours before the starting time. Over the next hour, both crews took the opportunity to practise a few starts and to try and dampen down the nerves and excitement that was beginning to build. A number of jazz bands had taken their place on the riverbank and Edwards could hear the jaunty music drifting over the river.

Stanley Baldwin, the Prime Minister and a keen follower of the sport, arrived with his wife and displayed his affiliation by taking up position within the Cambridge enclosure. The *Dundee Courier* reported, 'Mr Baldwin, who was smoking a cherrywood pipe, declined smilingly to say which crew he favoured'. Nobody was in any doubt though about his allegiance to the Light Blues.

With just an hour before the start, there was, as the *Daily Mail* stated, 'a kaleidoscopic view of a procession of all sorts of craft making their way upriver. There were barges and tugs on which were immaculately attired men and women, steam launches, luxurious motor boats and to complete the picture, dinghies hauled by the lusty watermen with full cargoes. All these churning the water into wavelets in their endeavours to get up stream in good time to view the race.'

Seated on one of the more luxurious motor launches was the exotic figure of Colonel Nawabzda Hamidullah Khan, the son of the Begum of Bhopal, and invited guest of the Prince of Wales. As all of these dignitaries and Old Blues made their way to the best vantage points on the river, the crews were trying their best to fight their nerves.

Sir James Croft sat with his crew in the boathouse and out of the windows they could see the vast crowds that had gathered. He recalled that, 'it almost felt as though we were to be sacrificed, that the crowd will gloat'.

Bossie Phelps took Sir James out in a launch for one final inspection of the conditions and the last instruction. 'It was always during this last run over that I realised how very imperfect my knowledge of the course was. I would return to the changing room, wondering furtively if there was no way out, and wishing heartily that I could suddenly get run down with a taxi and get an arm or a leg broken and thus escape'.

And then it was time to leave the boathouse and carry the boat down to the river. Hugh remembered, '...it was difficult to get through the crowd and one had plenty of time to read the posters carried by the religious sandwich men "Prepare to meet thy God" – which didn't help'.

The crew of the Oxford boat was, at a total of one hundred and ten stone, four stones the heavier of the two. Again, opinion was divided as to whether this provided Oxford with an advantage or not.

One advantage that Oxford did gain was in winning the toss of the coin. Oxford opted to take the Surrey shore but with the wind conditions so ideal it was difficult to ascertain any major advantage in winning that year's toss. One of the Cambridge coaches expressed the view that losing the toss was to their advantage as it would compel the Cambridge crew to go all out at the start in order to prevent Oxford gaining an immediate lead.

Being the challengers, the Oxford boat went afloat first, and to the accompaniment of a great cheer paddled away to the stake boats at the start. Even this manoeuvre is not at all easy – especially for Sir James as cox: 'Getting up to the stake boat is no easy feat. An eight is an awkward craft to turn, the tide is running very fast and there is not much room to spare. If you miss it, there is no chance of backing up to it, the tide is too strong.'

Both boats made it successfully to the stake boats, being held there by a waterman. Sweaters and scarves were removed, passed down the boat and deposited in the stake boat. The two crews were now poised, waiting for the umpire to lower his flag to signify the start. Sir James readied his crew. 'At that moment, as far as I was concerned at least, all fears departed. The crowd was forgotten, even the self-doubt that I never even knew the course properly was forgotten'.

The official starter held the flag aloft. On the opposite banks of the river, the crowd fell silent. At 12.26 p.m., the flag dropped. A tremendous cheer went up from the banks. The oars of the Oxford and Cambridge boats dug into the water, and both boats sprang forward simultaneously.

In the first minute, the Oxford crew found their rhythm quickly and went from ten, nineteen to thirty-seven strokes per minute for the twenty-second intervals. Cambridge, aware that they would need to ensure that Oxford did not draw away, responded with ten, nineteen to thirty-six strokes. Oxford had a slight lead, by a canvas, at the end of that first crucial minute.

In the second minute, the power of the heavier Oxford crew began to show and they were rowing thirty-two strokes to Cambridge's thirty, and had established a quarter length lead. This increased further to a lead of a third of a length at the Mile Post. This was reached by Oxford in four minutes and five seconds, a fast time considering the minimum of tide flowing in the Thames.

Vast crowds gather beside Hammersmith Bridge to watch the Oxford and Cambridge crews speed past, 1926, © Illustrated London News Group.

The Mile Post was the marker for Pitman, the Oxford stroke, to put in a spurt and to gain his boat a distinct lead over the Light Blues on the approach up to Hammersmith Bridge. Pitman increased his stroke rate and the crew followed him. Oxford's lead was now up to half a length but Cambridge were not to be shaken and Cambridge's stroke, Hamilton-Russell, responded.

Both boats were now rowing at a stroke rate of thirty and swept past the Harrods Depository. This was a crucial moment for Cambridge, this is where the Boat Race could be lost.

Cambridge had to ensure there was no clear water between themselves and Oxford as the approaching sharp bend of the river at Hammersmith would clearly benefit Oxford. At this crucial point Hugh heard Justin Brown, the Cambridge cox, bellow out: 'Oxford you are in my water. Give way you buggers. Croft, you c**t, get out of my water.'

Despite this being Croft's debut in the Boat Race – whereas the far more experienced Brown was on an unprecedented hat-trick of victories – he was well aware of his role: 'My job was to do the opposing cox down, to bluff him out of my way... a continuous flow of epithet passes. One

The Oxford crew for the Boat Race, as depicted by the cartoonist in The Tatler, March 31st, 1926, © Illustrated London News Group.

cox may know perfectly well that he is in his opponent's water, yet he will continue to warn him that unless he gives way he will foul him; the one with the best bluff wins and may in the first two miles of the race gain a very considerable advantage for his crew.'

The Oxford crew maintained their slim half a length lead as they reached Hammersmith Bridge in a time of seven minutes and twenty-seven seconds. Sir James Croft was steering the Oxford boat to perfection – as one old Oxford Blue remarked 'almost criminally well' – keeping Cambridge at bay.

Up to this point, despite the immense crowds lining the banks, the Oxford crew were unaware of any noise drifting over the water, they were concentrating fully on pulling the oars and keeping in front of Cambridge. But then a wall of noise avalanched across the water and over the boats. The hooters and sirens of all the factories on the banks were turned on to greet the boats. For Croft, this was the first time that he became aware that the boat was not going along in complete silence. 'One begins to realise that there are several hundreds of thousands of people on the bridges and along the banks, all using their lungs to make the most noise possible. The result can be best described as a dome of sound which seems to cover the river at an immense height like the dome of a cathedral.'

This dome of sound was at an unprecedented level in 1926 – nobody could remember a Boat Race that had been so tightly contested. This was a classic encounter. As the correspondent of *The Times* recounted, 'In no race since Bourne's famous race against Stewart in 1909, when they kept together till Dukes Meadows, have the crews rowed neck-and-neck together for such a large part of the course. Leads have changed in other races since then, right up to and after Barnes, but it is rarely one has the thrill of two crews rowing alongside for almost ten minutes.'

The crowd packed onto the Hammersmith Bridge were thrilled. Circling fifteen hundred feet above the river, and in a first for the Boat Race, was an Imperial Airways Handley-Page biplane chartered by a group of Cambridge supporters keen to view the race from a unique vantage point.

Oxford's winning of the toss had given them the advantage of the Surrey station and the bend of the river towards Chiswick steps. Sensing this was an opportune point to press home this advantage, Pitman put in another spurt. This time, his Oxford crew did not respond. Cambridge, realising that the bend was in Oxford's favour, also put on a spurt and the crew increased their stoke rate to thirty-two. This brought Cambridge level with the Oxford boat. The Oxford crew started to falter and, only just perceptibly, lose their rhythm. Oxford hung on, heading down the bend towards Chiswick.

Hamilton-Russell, the Cambridge cox, implored his crew to spurt in a series of 'tens' on the outside of the bend and suddenly, for the first time in the race, it was the Cambridge boat that edged ahead of their bitter rival. Then, as the *Evening Post* reported, 'approaching Chiswick steps, the race was marred by one of the greatest tragedies in the history of the event'.

As the Cambridge boat took the lead for the first time, the number six in the Oxford boat, James 'Spud' Thomson, glanced around at the passing Cambridge boat. Such a thing was not 'Etonian watermanship' and if he must look round, he did so over the wrong shoulder. Consequently, Thomson's rowing faltered badly and threw the rhythm of the crew out. Hugh, rowing at number five and seeing 'Spud' look round, cracked. He collapsed in the boat.

From the bank it looked to the spectators as if Oxford's number five had confusingly vanished. He was slumped backwards, fallen on the knees of 'Nono' Rathbone at number four, his oar dragging in the water. Rathbone shouted at Hugh to get up. With one hand, Rathbone managed to shove Hugh back into the sitting position. Sphinx, rowing at seven, was unaware that it was his brother who had ceased to row. Hugh collapsed once more. With the disarray in the Oxford boat, Cambridge shot ahead.

Two minutes after Hugh's collapse, the Cambridge boat had a three-length lead. The Oxford crew rowed on, as Croft recalled, 'like a creature with a broken back'. Rathbone pushed Hugh back into a sitting position and he finally came to. Hugh manfully gripped his oar and began to row once more.

At the three-mile mark Oxford were back rowing in rhythm at thirty strokes. But the race was lost. Cambridge's lead was now at four lengths. By the time the Oxford boat reached Barnes Bridge and the final slight bend into the finish, Cambridge were five lengths ahead.

Hugh, collapsed and lying prostrate at number five in the Oxford boat, at the end of the Boat Race.
Illustrated London News, *April 3rd, 1926, © Illustrated London News Group.*

The Cambridge boat finished in a time of nineteen minutes and twenty-nine seconds and won by five lengths.

In the British Pathé newsreel of the race, the boats are seen drifting past the finish marker. The Cambridge crew are triumphant but exhausted, and in the Oxford boat Hugh cannot be seen. He has once again slumped backwards into the boat. The closest Boat Race for seventeen years, up until the two-mile mark, turned into a non-contest. Cambridge had won, and for the newspapers the reason was simple: the inexcusable collapse of H. R. A. Edwards.

As the dejected Oxford crew waded ashore with their boat, a small boy broke free of the swarming crowd and approached Sir James Croft with an autograph book and a hopeful look on his face.

The reporters were gathered at the boat houses to obtain quotations to complement their race reports. In the *Sunday Post*, under the headline 'Disaster for Oxford', the Cambridge stroke, Hamilton-Russell, was quoted as, 'We were all very glad to win. However, I don't think I want to go through it again'.

Pitman, the Oxford stroke, was understandably upset: 'I am very sorry to have let the crew down'. As for Hugh, he was surrounded by the journalists desperate to find out what had happened in the boat. 'I felt groggy; that is all there is to it. But I tried to pull as best as I could for the last mile. I am fit again now, but for the moment everything was blurred.'

Cambridge's jubilant cox, celebrating his record third consecutive win, stated, 'I never doubted the issue after the crews had passed Hammersmith Bridge'. Cambridge had won seven of the last eight races.

The Times was the most scathing about Hugh and his collapse. The following day, in a summary of the events, the correspondent declared:

> 'Individuals in crews are allowed to eat too much and drink too much and are not made to work hard enough to keep themselves from getting fat. The result is they come to the post for the most gruelling athletic contest known in the world, not trained as a boxer would step into the ring, but overloaded with fat, which, in the first place, by being mistaken for muscle, leads one to expect more of them than one would of men of their true weight, and, secondly, by placing a dangerous strain on their heart renders them liable to collapse.'

Specifically about Hugh, *The Times* rowing correspondent continued:

> 'Number 5 in the Oxford crew was a young though not entirely inexperienced man, who was a good enough natural oar to be able to exhaust himself, which is a thing of which many heavyweights are too slow to be capable. He was never made to row hard during practice, and his weight was a stone too much. The Boat Race is not like a schoolboys' race, and a man must really be trained to undergo it or risk permanent injury to his health'.

After the race Guy Nickalls, the former Old Blue and Olympic gold medallist, referred directly to Hugh that he was more than a stone overweight and laden down with 'baby blubber'.

The Oxford crew, miserable and exhausted after their loss, were keen to stay indoors, away from the Press and the celebrations of Cambridge.

Sphinx tried to console his younger brother but realised his need for time alone. However, the crew had one further contractual commitment to fulfil – a trip to the cinema.

The crew arrived at the Rialto Theatre in the West End of London, to a packed audience, at 4 p.m. The European Film Company, the British subsidiary of Universal Pictures, had agreed the previous week with Oxford that the boat crew should be present at the cinema for a re-run of the race.

For the crew there could be nothing worse than to have to sit in the velvet seats of the Rialto, surrounded by a sell-out crowd of eight hundred, and watch their losing efforts. To make it even more of a traumatic experience, the Rialto in association with the *Daily Mail* had installed on the stage a large scenic panorama which showed, in model form and to scale, all the familiar vantage points such as the Fulham football ground, Harrods Depository and the bridges.

In the centre of this large panorama were two troughs of water, and in the two troughs a Light Blue boat and a Dark Blue boat. The *Daily Mail* installed their special 'Marconiphone' loud speakers which had recorded the crowd noise at over a dozen various points along the course, from Putney to Mortlake. From the time the crews embarked and left the bank to proceed to the starting stake, until Cambridge finished as the winners, the boats on the panorama moved simultaneously with those on the river, accompanied by movie clips from the race and the recorded cacophony of the crowds.

A newspaper of the time, *The Bioscope*, noted that the Oxford crew were 'immensely interested and at once saw where they cracked. The whole sporting spirit of the beaten crew was shown when they all stood up and cheered when Cambridge went over the line as winners'. Surrounded by a sell-out audience, it was the only option open to the crew.

In a concluding paragraph, *The Bioscope* went on: 'It was noticed on arrival that Number 5, Mr Edwards, was still in a very exhausted condition'.

Boat Race Night was a traditionally raucous evening in London. In the stories of P. G. Wodehouse, Bertie Wooster revels in the excitement of Boat Race nights in the 1920s, referring to them as a time of riotous celebration. In Wodehouse's short story 'Without the Option', published in *The Strand* magazine in June 1925, Bertie Wooster 'lets himself go' on Boat Race night and ends up in court accused, along with his friend Oliver 'Sippy' Sipperley, of stealing a policeman's helmet.

> 'Boat race night was a night of carnival in the West End, the exuberance incidental to each recurring anniversary of the great river festival was no less marked this year than on similar previous occasions. In the hotels, theatres, and the public streets merriment held undisputed sway. Early in the evening motor cars and taxicabs decorated with the colours of the rival crews careered gaily through the many thoroughfares packed inside and outside with boisterous revellers, while no less enthusiastic roisterers thronged the pavements. The fun was heightened by the weird headgear and grotesque garb here and there worn, accompanied in many instances by false noses of purple hue and the familiar beaver beard. To add to the hilarity large numbers of demonstrators paraded the streets armed with rattles, trumpets, and other noisy instruments, which were more cheerful than melodious. As the night wore on the crowds increased in volume. At several hotels and restaurants special celebrations of the event were arranged. Light and dark blue fairy lights twinkled at the tables, and ballrooms resounded with joyous dancing to the lilting jazz music of perspiring bandsmen. It was a night of unrestrained conviviality, and not until after midnight did the crowds disperse, and the strains of merriment die away.' (*The Scotsman, March 30th, 1925*)

To the great relief of the police, the night was a rare uneventful evening of disorder: there were only fifty arrests. As with Bertie Wooster, a great many of those arrests resulted in fines for drunkenness and disorderly conduct.

Hugh returned to Oxford bitterly disappointed by the loss and his part in it. He was sent to the College doctor to be examined.

'The doctor who examined me afterwards with the aid of X-ray plates told me that due to a dilated heart I must never again take any strenuous exercise, and in bidding me adieu he extended to me his best wishes for my gaining a "blue" in crown bowls'.

His rowing days were over. Hugh was distraught.

Looking back on the race many years later, Hugh conceded that 'with the lack of any additional exercise, which I always needed, I put on too much weight and was far from fit at the end of training'.

Despite this soul searching, there was also a lingering anger at the Press for putting so much of the blame on his shoulders. 'Though I deserved every word of it, I was pretty disgusted with the press I received, especially from *The Times*. I was bitterly disappointed, but this was primarily for letting down my crew, and especially my brother Sphinx.'

There was one former rower and coach who did defend Hugh in the newspaper. Steve Fairbairn, who would soon become such an important figure in his life, wrote in the newspapers that Hugh was not the one to blame.

'The one person who showed kindness, if not truthfulness, was Steve Fairbairn who wrote that I had been pulling the whole boat along for the first two miles.'

These few words of kindness from Steve Fairbairn gave Hugh something to cling to.

Chapter 5

Leaving Oxford

With his rowing career at an end, Hugh had to turn his attention to his academic studies. The devastation at the medical prognosis and the effect of all the press scrutiny resulted in Hugh finding it difficult to concentrate at his studies. The thought of playing crown bowls did not appeal.

Hugh had also lost his father in January 1927. Reverend Edwards had not taken to the city life of Oxford, and felt it was his duty to be back in the countryside preaching to the villagers. He accepted the position of vicar for St Denys, Northmoor, and moved into the Oxfordshire vicarage. Tragically his happiness was curtailed by ill-health. 'My father died, no doubt as a result of the damp, unhealthy climate of Northmoor and my mother soon left the vicarage and bought a house in Kensington, London, close to her beloved church of St John's.'

Hugh would often take solitary walks through the Christ Church meadows and up to the river. He would sit watching the oarsmen and their coaches. Rowing was his passion, and the draw was irresistible.

Tentatively, he plucked up the courage to borrow a sculling boat from the Christ Church boat house. It was an early morning, and the river was quiet. Hugh clambered into the boat and sat silently, listening to the water beneath him. He took hold of the wooden oars and closed his eyes.

The memories of sculling on the Thames as a schoolboy, trying to match the stroke rate of Jack Beresford, flooded back. With a deep breath he began to row. Would his dilated heart take the strain?

The depression that had settled on Hugh was lifted as soon as he was back in a boat. In the first few weeks of Spring he would tentatively row himself gently down the river and back. Finding to his immense relief that he felt no ill-effects he was soon increasing his stroke rate. Over the Summer months he spent as much time as he could rebuilding his fitness and confidence in his body.

In Hugh's mind, he was now ready to be selected to row in the Christ Church summer eight, which was Head of the River. The coaches refused to select him, and it was then that realisation dawned on him.

'What the doctor told me about my health was merely a kind and polite way of letting me know that I was no longer required as an oarsman in any crew.'

Hugh did not have a dilated heart. The College thought it best that he quietly gave up on rowing, and instead recommended that he transfer his efforts from rowing a boat into coaching a crew. His collapse in the Boat Race was an embarrassment to those who had selected him in the first place. This slight just added to an already smouldering desire to prove everyone wrong.

Returning to Oxford in the Michaelmas term after the long Summer vacation, Hugh entered the Christ Church regatta single sculls event. To the shock of the spectators, he made it to the final. Awaiting him was the talented R. T. Lee (Worcester College) who the following year would go on to win the Diamonds at Henley.

Several of those witnessing the final commented that they fully expected to see Edwards collapse once more and feared for his well-being. Hugh won the race by a length.

Almost eight months to the day from the calamity of the Boat Race, Hugh was once again victorious in a boat.

Leaving Oxford

At the end of the Trinity term Hugh sat his exams.

In his own admission, 'One of the bugbears of University life is that you have to take examinations from time to time. I eagerly went along when the results were posted, but my name was not listed among those who had satisfied the examiners, not even in a single subject'.

His only hope was to re-sit the exams at the end of the Michaelmas term and to achieve a pass. Just after he retook the exams, but before the term had ended, Hugh received a note from the Proctors stating that he had been seen in the Carfax Assembly Rooms dancing 'with a lady from the Town' and inviting him to attend the Clarendon Buildings the following morning.

There was a very sharp line drawn between 'Gown' and 'Town'. 'Gown' comprised all the gentlemen and ladies of the University, while 'Town' encapsulated all the rest who lived in Oxford. Undergraduates were not permitted to mix in any way with the latter. There was an additional problem for Hugh. If you went to a dance, inevitably you had to surreptitiously climb, literally, back into College afterwards, and this was a challenge that he welcomed.

'There were reputed to be several ways in, but I knew only one. I climbed over the railings in the Merton Street entrance to the Meadows and then over the wall into the college grounds. From there, I scaled the wall into Canon Locke's garden, shinned up a convenient tree to mount the 10-foot wall of Meadow Buildings and then dropped down on to the roof of the bicycle shed and so to the ground. The Meadow porter was waiting for me. I was in double trouble.'

Hugh declined the invitation to the meeting with the Proctors and, telling the Senior Proctor, Mr Chaundry, exactly where he could put his gown Hugh walked out of Oxford.

Chapter 6

Jumbo Arises

Employment was hard to come by in 1927 and Hugh moved back to live with his mother in Kensington. Britain's economy was still struggling to pay for the effects of the First World War and recovering from the General Strike of the previous year. Hugh's initial thought for a future life was of emigrating to one of the Dominions to take up sheep farming. Hugh obtained all the information he could on the merits of merino sheep but failed to raise the capital required to travel. So, to ease his boredom, he spent most of his time sculling on the river.

Hugh was a member of both London Rowing Club and its rival Thames Rowing Club. Julius 'Old Man Berry' Beresford – Jack's father – approached Edwards and asked, 'would you like to row in our Thames Cup eight?'. The reply was a polite, but short, 'No thanks, Berry'. Hugh was not about to be lured back to a life dedicated to competitive rowing.

In the mid-1920s, Thames Rowing Club had been successful under the aegis of their Australian-born coach Steve Fairbairn. However, it had been split into two factions: those who were disciples of Fairbairn and those who favoured the more traditional coaching of Julius Beresford. Amidst the in-fighting, Fairbairn decided to quit Thames and was immediately asked to coach at their bitter rivals London. The captain of London was

Robert 'Archie' Nisbet, a great admirer of Steve Fairbairn, and when Fairbairn accepted the offer several of his disciples came over with him.

After a leisurely afternoon scull on the river – and much to his surprise – Nisbet approached Hugh with a proposition. Nisbet invited Hugh to row in the London Rowing Club Grand eight. Remembering the kind words that Steve Fairbairn had told the Press after the Boat Race, Edwards accepted the invitation. If Fairbairn had faith in him after his collapse, then he would put his faith in Fairbairn.

From that day, Edwards did not set foot in the Thames Rowing Club for over twenty years.

The rivalry between the two clubs was not a friendly one.

'We did not have a good word to say of each other and, when the opportunity offered, were distinctly unkind to our rivals. In the evenings Thames men had to walk past the London boathouse and we would stand on the balcony and jeer as they went past. John Badcock was the mainstay of the Thames Grand eight, so we would pick him out as our main target, but it annoyed us that he never looked up but just kept on walking, always immaculately dressed and complete with bowler hat, tightly rolled umbrella and a copy of *The Times* under his arm. In fact, he reminded us of the cartoon character Felix the Cat and the nickname stuck. After marrying Joyce Cooper, the Olympic swimmer, they christened their eldest son Felix.'

For Edwards, it felt momentous when he first stepped into the London eight with Steve Fairbairn alongside in the launch. Unlike his experience at Oxford, Edwards was of the strong opinion that he had found his true home.

'Rowing in that crew was an absolute delight. The rhythm set by Terence O'Brien at stroke was out of this world, the smoothness, power, balance and control were the epitome of poetry of motion.'

His experience of being coached under Fairbairn was equally uplifting.

'Unlike "orthodox" coaches who were always nagging about little points of style, Steve said very little, and never seemed to address an individual, but spoke to the crew as a whole. During one whole outing he might repeat at intervals, "Sit back at the finish; sit back till the cows come home". On another trip it would be "Round the turn, just like turning mother's mangle", "If you cannot do it easy, you cannot do it at all", and "Mileage makes Champions".'

Fairbairn worked the crew hard, and each man in the crew vied with the others in 'sending down the biggest and truest puddle'. Fairbairn would work with both the first and second eights, handicapping the crews so that the Grand eight would go ahead in the last few hundred yards.

Hugh recalled, 'I asked him one day in the club about a point of technique when he grabbed me at waist level by the sweater and said, "This is the way to finish the stroke" at the same time flinging me across the room. I was no wiser than I was before, but I pondered on the episode for a long time. Shortly after, Ted Phelps was brought into the boat at number six to substitute for a man who was sick. I noticed Ted's outside shoulder coming at me like a sledgehammer at the finish of the stroke, and at last I understood what Steve meant.'

Under the guidance of Fairbairn, Hugh had fallen back in love with the art of rowing. When the London eight took to the water, he could at last truly hear the boat sing.

In 1927 the London eight won every race they entered, home and abroad, save only the Grand and Stewards' at Henley Royal Regatta. As well as the teaching methods of Fairbairn, Edwards was driven by a sense of redemption: 'Victory would begin to teach Guy Nickalls and the rest of the Leander pink-cap brigade to talk about "baby blubber".'

It was in the London eight that Edwards would acquire his nickname.

'In the London crew I was placed in the middle of the boat being twelve stone nine pounds, one of the heavyweights. Put at number four was 'Fatty' Webb turning the scales at twelve stone ten pounds. The day came when my weight went up to twelve stone and eleven pounds and Fatty went down to twelve stones and eight pounds. Webb proudly declared,

"You are a lump; you are nothing but a jumbo". And the name stuck.'

From this point on he would always be known within rowing circles as 'Jumbo'. It is unknown whether Webb was still referred to as 'Fatty'.

The newly christened 'Jumbo' Edwards had rediscovered his passion, but a life spent rowing was not viable. He needed to find work.

At the end of 1927 he was approached through a family friend to become an assistant schoolmaster at Courtenay Lodge School for Boys. The salary was a rather paltry £100 per year, but it was paid employment and as well as teaching the boys in English, mathematics and history there was an opportunity to coach the senior boys in rowing.

The school was located in Sutton Courtenay, south of Oxford, and very close to the Thames and so Jumbo could row in what spare time he had. At weekends he would dash back to London on his Norton motorbike and continue his coaching under Steve Fairbairn. The London Rowing Club eight were building towards Henley and another shot at the pinnacle of winning the Grand.

The rivalry with Thames Rowing Club was as intense as ever, and there were also battles on the river with the venerable Leander Club.

As Jumbo articulated in his book *The Way of a Man with a Blade,* the London crew had a huge respect for Leander but this was coupled with contempt as they were of the 'wrong faith'. Leander was an adherent to the school of 'Orthodoxy' when it came to their rowing technique, whereas Steve Fairbairn had created such a unique technique that this was now commonly referred to as 'Fairbairnism'.

The orthodox system called for a series of highly regimented and rigid body motions; Fairbairn's stroke emphasized the whole of the stroke rather than individual components with the intent of smoothly and organically sending one's 'puddles' as far to the stern as possible – 'the water boiling aft'. Fairbairn's innovation was to concentrate the oarsman's mind on moving the boat rather than on the supposedly correct motions of the body.

There was something of the mystic in Fairbairn's search for perfection in rowing. For Jumbo, 'it was a disgrace to be beaten by a crew rowing the orthodox way'. However, this is exactly what happened in the final of the Grand at Henley in 1927 – Thames won by three quarters of a length.

Despite this bitter defeat, the London crew were improving month by month, year by year. The boat was getting faster. The crew possessed that *esprit de corps* that was so vital to compete against the best crews in the world.

Chapter 7
Henley Hat-trick

Throughout 1928 and 1929, Jumbo continued his role as assistant schoolmaster whilst travelling to London each weekend to row. His passion for rowing was as intense as ever, but a new love was developing.

In 1927 his brother Sphinx, along with Sir James Croft as cox, competed once more in the Boat Race. It was not to be third time lucky for Sphinx as Oxford lost again to Cambridge. This time the Light Blues won by three lengths and Oxford were overhauled at that all too familiar point at Chiswick Steps.

On graduation from Christ Church, Sphinx opted to join the fledgling Royal Air Force. Both brothers were to fall in love with flying planes. Jumbo decided that the life of a schoolmaster held little appeal when compared to the thrills of taking to the skies in the biplanes of the day. He quickly learnt the basics of how to get an aeroplane into the air, and safely back again, and longed to follow his brother into the RAF. The only problem was that to obtain a permanent commission in the RAF as a pilot you had to get a University degree and a University Commission. There was only one option for Jumbo, a return to Oxford and his studies.

To even be considered by Oxford, Jumbo had to pass his entrance exams and with a lot of effort and long hours of study he achieved just that. However, there was the issue of the letter that Jumbo had written to the

Senior Proctor three years ago. The letter had not been forgotten. The College informed Jumbo that he would have to apologise formally before acceptance back into the academic confines of Christ Church. A letter of apology was carefully worded by Jumbo and he found himself once more back in Oxford.

The Oxford University Boat Club had followed Jumbo's remarkable rowing progress over the past couple of years. Realising that rowing was not going to kill him, Jumbo was invited back into the Varsity boat to take on the near invincibility of Cambridge in the 1930 Boat Race.

Having become a dedicated disciple to Fairbairnism and still rowing for London, Jumbo did not want to go back into the Oxford boat and row in the orthodox coaching method. He also did not want to waste his time with the demands of the intensive practice; his new aim in life was to obtain his degree which would allow him to join the RAF.

Alastair Graham, the President of Oxford, refused to take no as an answer and wanted Jumbo back in their eight.

'In the end I explained that having rowed under Steve Fairbairn for a few years I could not now go back to the orthodox style and row with fixed oarlocks. I finished up by saying that I would row in the crew only if I could have a swivel rowlock. This impossible condition would, I thought, put an end to the President's importuning. He said, "That's splendid. We will fix you up with swivel straight away". I found myself in the crew.'

Dr Pat Mallam, one of the Oxford coaches, also approached Jumbo to encourage him to return to the boat in his usual position at number five.

'It was in vain that I told him I not only wanted to work for my degree, but I also wished to fly with the Air Squadron. He continued to plead with me until finally in desperation I said "To tell you the truth, Pat, I can't row because I am only just recovering from a nasty dose of syphilis". Pat replied sharply, "Balls Jumbo, I am the VD doctor for Oxford, and I know you are not". I had no more ammunition and so found myself in the boat, but I was not very happy about it because it had been such a joy to me rowing under Steve Fairbairn for London Rowing Club, under the leadership of that incomparable stroke, Terence O'Brien'

After his collapse in 1926, Jumbo was unexpectedly back in the Oxford boat for the 1930 Boat Race.

At number six in the Varsity crew was a fellow Christ Church rower and Etonian, Lewis Clive. This was the first time that Jumbo and Lewis rowed together, and it was the start of a partnership that would develop into one of the most formidable – and successful – coxless pairs that the country had produced.

This Edwards and Clive partnership within the Dark Blue eight was to no avail. Cambridge, for the seventh year in a row, won the Boat Race.

The 1930 Boat Race was a lot closer than when Jumbo collapsed in 1926. Despite Oxford leading past the ill-fated Chiswick Steps, Cambridge proved the stronger of the two and won by two lengths in a time of nineteen minutes and nine seconds.

Once more Stanley Baldwin, now Leader of the Opposition, watched on in satisfaction – puffing on his cherry wood pipe – as his favoured Light Blues crossed the line.

The disappointment of losing was intense for Jumbo, but unlike three years previously there was no feeling of humiliation or personal disaster.

The rowing correspondent of *The Times* was not prepared to provide any redemptive words to ease the pain of Jumbo's loss. 'Edwards is not at his best again even now, and his form suffered at the end of Saturday's long row. His finish when he is tired is the worst in the crew. He snatches his blade home with his elbows out, a heritage of Metropolitan rowing.'

Jumbo returned to his beloved London Rowing Club crew, and once again embraced the Fairbairn methodology. The Christ Church partnership with Lewis Clive also evolved into an effective pair. The two continued to row together with the aim of participating at Henley in the Silver Goblets & Nickalls' Challenge Cup.

The Oxford eight for the Boat Race, 1930. Lewis Clive (back row, left) alongside Hugh (back row, middle).

Initially, Jumbo had his doubts. 'After the Boat Race defeat, Lewis Clive asked me to row in a pair with him. I was not terribly keen because, although he had a valiant heart and the strength of a horse, he was a little bit clumsy, surprising in an Eton boy.'

Four months after the loss in the Boat Race, it was the Henley Regatta. London Rowing Club had entered their eight for the Grand and the four for the Stewards'. Jumbo was selected for both crews, and he also entered the Diamond Challenge Sculls. However, it was too soon in Jumbo's partnership with Lewis Clive for the Christ Church pair to compete for the Silver Goblets.

It was a gruelling task for any rower to compete in three world-class events but at the age of twenty-three, and having rowed extensively over the past four years, Jumbo was in the best form of his life.

As Jumbo recounted, 'For most of the oarsman the two weeks of Henley was not merely the Mecca of their ambitions; it was their annual holiday as well. These two mutually antagonistic aims had to be very carefully blended by the coach. We worked to a very strict daily routine.'

07.15	Get up. Cup of milk and a biscuit
07.20	Run up Remenham Hill
08.00	Breakfast
10.00	Answering nature's call in the Pink Palace (Leander Boat house)
10.45	Afloat! Practice on the course
12.00	Stewards' IV afloat for practice
13.00	Lunch
14.15	Bed
15.45	Tea
17.15	Afloat for practice
18.30	Stewards' IV afloat for practice
20.00	Dinner
22.15	Bed

The answering of nature's call in Leander was symbolic of what the London crew intended to do to their rival crew in the regatta.

In the Diamond Challenge Sculls heats, Jumbo had a tough draw against the Canadian John 'Jack' Guest of the Argonaut Rowing Club. Jack Guest had won a silver medal in the double sculls at the Olympic Games of 1928, and his experience easily put paid to Jumbo's hopes. After defeating Jumbo, Jack would go on to win that year's Diamond Challenge Sculls.

Jumbo's defeat in the sculls did allow him to concentrate on the eight and four, and the London crew progressed easily through the heats and made the final of both the Grand and the Stewards'. Their opponents in both finals were Leander.

The Grand Challenge Cup was the prize that London valued the most. It had been forty years – since 1890 – that London had last won this prestigious trophy, and now it was only Leander between them and a vindication of their 'Metropolitan' training methods under Fairbairn.

'We had been waiting for this opportunity for years', recalled Jumbo. 'This year there was no doubt about our superiority, but we had to think of the years to come. We had to demonstrate, to all the rowing community, our complete supremacy.'

It was pointed out to Jumbo prior to the race that, once again, Stanley Baldwin was in the enclosure.

London's plan was to row as fast as possible to the Barrier (a point reached in two minutes) and then put in a mighty spurt. 'All went absolutely to plan; we romped away from Leander and were two lengths up at the end of the spurt.'

However, this was not the conventional way for an eight to try and win the race. A lead of two lengths in two minutes resulted in the London eight skimming down the river one foot per second faster than Leander. The drag of an eight increases as the square of the speed, so London had to expend an incredible amount of power to achieve that speed. London had burnt themselves up to purely demonstrate their supremacy over Leander. 'We were unable to continue that pace and dropped down to a rate that we could only just manage', Jumbo recalled. 'To the onlooker – including my nemesis Stanley Baldwin – it looked, no doubt, as though we were playing with Leander, dropping to a paddle and allowing them to come back at us. If so, we attained our aim.'

The London crew won by a full length and a half. Terence O'Brien was handed the trophy by Fred Fenner – who had rowed in the last London winning crew in 1862.

London Rowing Club had finally regained the Grand trophy, forty years from the date that they were last triumphant.

Later that same day, Jumbo rowed to another victory in the London four - and the Stewards' trophy was captured to go with the Grand. Once again, the vanquished crew was Leander and the victory was a length and a half. Fairbairnism had triumphed over Orthodox.

The Times rowing correspondent finally penned an article that praised Jumbo. 'The outstanding individuals in the Regatta were H. R. A. Edwards, the number five of the London crew, and A. Graham, number seven in the Leander crew. For power, skill, and smoothness combined Edwards stands alone among the heavyweights of today, and it is a pleasure to be able to pay such a tribute to one who had earned it in the face of considerable difficulty.'

Redemption was sweet.

With so much success in July 1930, the London crew had hoped to relax away from the river but this was not to be. The eight and four were selected to represent England in the 1930 British Empire Games, to be held across the Atlantic in Hamilton, Ontario. This was the very first British Empire Games, later to become known as the Commonwealth Games.

In July 1929, Jumbo had successfully passed his flying exam and had been issued with his Private Pilot's Certificate and Licence from the Air Ministry. To qualify for his licence, Jumbo had joined the London Aeroplane Club at the de Havilland Aerodrome, Stag Lane, where one of his flight instructors was Captain Valentine Henry Baker MC, AFC – a former First World War fighter pilot. One of Jumbo's fellow pupils was Amy Johnson – who the following year would go on to worldwide fame as the first woman to fly solo from Great Britain to Australia.

Jumbo would arrive for rowing practice by flying his Avro Baby airplane to Molesey, in Surrey, land on the nearby racecourse and amble along the couple of hundred yards to the boathouse.

At the beginning of August 1930, London Rowing Club crew boarded the *Empress of Australia* and crossed the Atlantic to Canada. The London crew kept themselves fit by running around the deck and exercising in the first-class swimming pool and gymnasium.

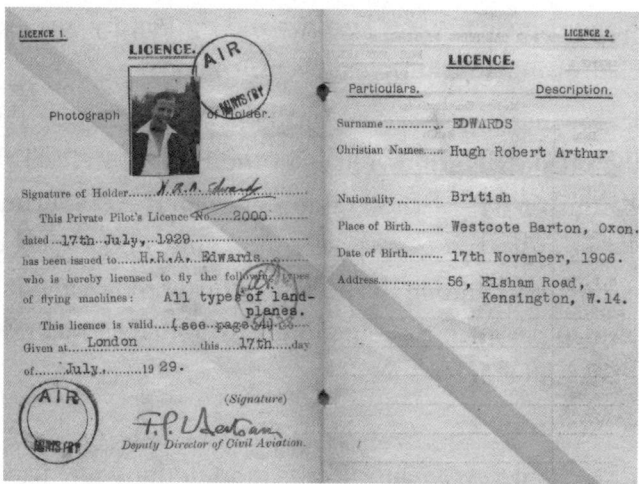

The private pilot's licence (number 2000) issued to Hugh in July 1929.

Despite the long voyage, the all-conquering crew were again triumphant and were proving themselves on the international stage. They won both of their finals and proudly wore two gold medals around their necks.

A triumphant Jumbo recalled that, 'We won the eights and the coxless fours, and the New Zealanders were terribly surprised and most upset that they had not won. The stroke of our eight was Terence O'Brien, the most magnificent stroke it has ever been my privilege to follow.'

In 1931, the London crew continued their supremacy on water. In the Spring of that year, Lewis Clive had approached Jumbo with the idea of the two of them to team up once more in the coxless pairs – with the ultimate aim of winning the Silver Goblets at Henley. Victory at Henley in the pairs would result in them being noticed and potentially in the running to be selected for the following year's Olympic Games in Los Angeles.

Jumbo was now devoting much of his rowing time to the pairs partnership with Lewis and was fearful that London would not select him for the eight or four at Henley. His fear was unfounded and at Henley he was competing in the Grand, the Stewards' and the Goblets.

'For me, it meant six sessions per day, in the morning first the eights and then the fours and finally the pair, and the same thing in the evening.'

In the eight, London had lost one vital member of the crew. 'Our eight was not as good as the previous year, as we had lost our stroke Terry O'Brien who had got himself married. Kitty had given Terry an ultimatum, to choose "between me or rowing". Sadly for us, Terry chose Kitty.'

After defeating the American challenge of Harvard University in the heats, the semi-final of the Grand was against the formidable Berliner Rowing Club of Germany. This would turn out to be one of the finest races that Henley had witnessed for many a year.

At the Mile Post, Berlin were up by a quarter of a length. Edgar Howitt, the replacement at stroke for O'Brien, increased the stroke rate of the London eight to forty. This had the desired effect and the crew raced up to the enclosures with the Germans a narrow canvas ahead, but London could not get level. 'One hundred yards from the finish the Germans faltered, slightly, for one stroke but still remained a few feet ahead. Two lengths from the finishing post they blew up and we went past, ourselves blowing up one length short of the post and drifting over the line. I doubt if ever such an extraordinary scene had been witnessed at Henley. The crowds were beside themselves with excitement and joy.'

In retelling this victory, Jumbo omits to mention if Stanley Baldwin was looking on.

In a preliminary of the Stewards' Challenge Cup for fours, London Rowing Club met a familiar rival – though this time it was to be Thames Rowing Club and not Leander. In a punishing race, the London four were pushed all the way by Thames but managed to hold off a final spurt from their rivals and win by a third of a length.

In the final of the Stewards', London defeated the Italian challenge of Piacenza.

Alongside Lewis Clive, a tired but determined Jumbo completed a Henley hat-trick with victory in the Goblets against Kingston Rowing

The Duchess of York presenting a hat-trick of Henley victories for Hugh, 1931. Top: London Rowing Club eight awarded the Grand Challenge Cup; Below left: London Rowing Club four accepting the Stewards' Challenge Cup; Below right: Lewis and Hugh representing Christ Church are victorious in the Silver Goblets & Nickalls' Challenge Cup.

Club. This feat was almost unprecedented. 'Nobody had won three open events at Henley since Claude Taylor had achieved the feat in 1907, and nobody has achieved it since. Though for me it was quite a strenuous day, I have never before felt quite so fit.' To this day, no rower has again matched Jumbo's achievement at Henley.

The Henley prizes were presented by the Duchess of York. The third time Jumbo came up to the dais to receive his Silver Goblet, she smiled warmly. 'Fancy seeing you again Mr Edwards. Very many congratulations.'

Five years on from the depths of despair and humiliation, Jumbo Edwards had triumphantly scaled the heights of rowing at the world's most prestigious regatta. By this point, in the Summer of 1931, the Press had finally recognised that Jumbo was one of the finest rowers that the country had produced.

As well as finding redemption in the newspapers, Jumbo also received a compliment from the redoubtable Guy Nickalls.

'I felt I was now in a position to forgive Guy and his talk of "baby fat", and that regatta of 1931 saw the end of my resentment to the aftermath of 1926.'

Having finally graduated from Oxford, Jumbo had successfully applied for a commission with the Royal Air Force. However, there was one more rowing challenge on the horizon – Los Angeles and the Xth Olympic Games.

Chapter 8

Fastest Pair in the World

Lewis Clive was born on September 8th, 1910. His father, Percy Archer Clive, had earlier that year been re-elected as Member of Parliament for Ross – a county constituency centred on the town of Ross-on-Wye in Herefordshire. Percy's life had been primarily a military one. After an education at Eton, Percy enrolled at the Royal Military College, Sandhurst, and shortly after he was commissioned into the Grenadier Guards. While fighting in the Second Boer War, he stood as the Liberal Unionist Party candidate for the Ross constituency in the 'khaki election' of 1900. He was unopposed in the election and so was duly elected, for the first time, to the Commons as the MP for Ross.

Percy's priority was serving his country in South Africa. He did not return to England to take his seat in the Commons until February 1902, having been wounded in the fighting. In June that year he was appointed as Private Secretary for Parliamentary purposes to Lord George Hamilton, Secretary of State for India. Percy was unseated at the 1906 general election, narrowly losing the seat by just three hundred and twelve votes to the Liberal candidate, Alan Gardner.

Just two years later, on the death of Gardner, Percy returned to Parliament with victory in the by-election of January 1908. Percy successfully defended the seat twice in the General Elections of 1910, but when the

First World War broke out, and with Lewis just four years of age, he once again returned to the Grenadier Guards as Lieutenant Colonel. His wife, Alice, commonly known as Muriel, whom Percy had married in 1905, started plans to open a hospital for the casualties they knew would soon follow.

On April 5th, 1918, Percy was killed in action at Bucquoy, a small village south of Arras in Northern France. He was shot whilst rescuing a fallen comrade. He was awarded the Legion of Honour and was one of twenty-two Members of Parliament who died during the First World War. Eight days later, Jumbo's uncle, Thomas Pryce, was killed whilst fighting with the Grenadier Guards to repel the same German Spring Offensive.

Lewis was only seven years old when his father was killed in the war. He was brought up on the family Herefordshire estate with three sisters, one elder and two younger, and an elder brother. Mourning the loss of his father, Lewis dedicated himself to his studies and took up rowing at Eton. While at Eton, Clive unusually held two of the most prestigious posts in the school, that of Captain of the Oppidans – selected as he was one of the older boys at school – and Captain of Boats. As with Jumbo, Lewis was keen to enrol at Christ Church after leaving Eton due to the excellence of their boat house.

It was here, in 1930, that Jumbo and Lewis first met. Their inclusion in the Oxford crew for the Boat Race of 1930 did not result in success against the dominant Light Blues of Cambridge, but whilst Lewis continued his studies at Christ Church, and Jumbo rowed with London, they remained in touch and would go rowing together.

In the Easter holidays, shortly after the loss in the Boat Race, Lewis asked Jumbo if he wouldn't mind flying him up to Whitfield House – his family home in Herefordshire. As Jumbo recalled: 'Lewis was a big, heavy man. On our first attempt to take off from Hendon, my Avro failed to take to the skies. On the second shot I raised the tail extra high, with the prop only just clearing the grass, and we just cleared the fence at the aerodrome boundary.'

Although Jumbo had his doubts about the 'clumsiness' of Lewis in a boat, his strength and heart were not in any doubt. On their first outing as a pair they were hailed from the tow path by one of the Christ Church coaches, Pat Mallam. 'That is awfully good. You ought to go for the Goblets. But, Clive, you must swing a little straighter and arch your inside wrist more.'

Ever after, Mallam was to claim that he coached the pair to their future success.

1932 was an Olympic year. With his spectacular triple triumph at Henley in 1931, Jumbo's thoughts were turning to the host city of the Summer Olympic Games: Los Angeles.

The Olympic Games were scheduled to take place in the first couple of weeks in August. As with previous Summer Games, the selection of the rowers for the Great Britain team was reliant on the form displayed at Henley Royal Regatta. Henley was at the beginning of July. This left just over two weeks to when the British athletes had to set sail for the United States.

London Rowing Club looked to repeat their spectacular successes of 1931 at Henley, but they failed to defend their titles in the Grand or the Stewards'. They were defeated in the heats of the Stewards' by the Berliner Rowing Club of Germany and – in the heats of the Grand – Leander got their revenge. The Leander team that year consisted of the winning eight from Cambridge that had contested the Boat Race, and with this victory they were assured of their selection for the journey out to Los Angeles.

For Jumbo, his last chance of Henley glory and a ticket to America was in the coxless pairs with Lewis – to defend the Silver Goblets that they had won the previous year.

The pair progressed easily through the heats, but there was to be a dramatic semi-final. Awaiting Jumbo and Lewis were the talented Offer brothers of Kingston Rowing Club – who also targeted Henley as a golden opportunity to gain Olympic selection.

Lewis (front) and Hugh out on the river for a practice row, 1932.

Dick and Jack Offer were an experienced pairing and as holders of the Gentlemen's Double Sculls at the Skiff Championships Regatta the contest was going to be close. It was: the semi-final ended in a dead heat. Not since 1911 had the finishing line adjudicators been unable to separate two crews. A re-row was required, and this time the strength and endurance of Jumbo and Lewis was the deciding factor. At the Mile Post, Dick Offer collapsed and Jumbo and Lewis paddled home for an easy victory.

In the final of the Silver Goblets, Jumbo and Lewis rowed to victory by three lengths over W. H. Migotti and J. H. Lascelles of Gordouli Boat Club, Balliol College, Oxford. They had retained the Silver Goblets, and two days later on July 5th, the British team for the Olympics was announced.

As expected, the Cambridge eight that were triumphant in the Boat Race and had rowed to victory in the Leander colours at Henley were selected: Tom Askwith, David Haig-Thomas, Lewis Luxton, Donald McCowen, Kenneth Payne, Harold Rickett, Bill Sambell and the cox Charles Sergel.

For the coxless four, Thames Rowing Club crew got the nod ahead of their rivals, London. Victory at Henley was the impetus behind the selectors decision to opt for the Thames four: John 'Felix' Badcock, Thomas 'Tig' Tyler, Rowland George and Jack Beresford. At the age of thirty-three, this would be Jack's fourth consecutive Olympic Games.

Understandably, there was no place for Jumbo in the four or the eight. However, with their dominance at Henley, it was no surprise that Jumbo and Lewis were chosen to represent Great Britain in the coxless pairs. For the single sculls, Dick Southwood – Jack Beresford's protégé at Thames Rowing Club – was picked.

In just fifteen days' time Jumbo and Lewis would be boarding a ship to cross the Atlantic, and then onward to California.

For many, the chance to represent your country in an Olympic Games would be the pinnacle of a sporting life. Jumbo though felt slightly indifferent to the honour of selection for the Great Britain team.

'Come to think of it, looking back my selection was quite extraordinary, but, though I was terribly keen to see more of the 'New World', I was quite indifferent about the Olympic Games. We were quite certain that we were the fastest pair in the world. It did not seem necessary to go six thousand miles to prove it.'

For both Jumbo and Lewis, as well as all the other British rowers in the early and mid-part of the 20th Century, the apex of rowing excellence was Henley Royal Regatta – not the Olympic Games. Henley had been established in 1839, whilst rowing had only made its debut as an Olympic sport thirty-two years previously at the Paris Games of 1900. Rowing was included in the programme for the inaugural 1896 Olympic Games in Athens, but the competition was cancelled due to rough conditions on the course at Piraeus.

With their dominance at Henley over the past two years, their confidence was so high that Jumbo was certain that they were unbeatable. Complacency was to be their greatest fear.

The assurance that the pair exuded was justified. Not only were they considered the foremost pairing in the country with regards to ability, their sheer strength and determination was often cited by the coaches as the difference between them and those that they vanquished. This was evidenced in their Henley semi-final re-row victory against the Offer brothers.

For Jumbo, strength and determination were important but it was the 'art of rowing' that was his passion. 'As an oarsman I had never worried my head about the theory of rowing, only the art. All I was interested in was moving the boat fast and winning races, and to this end I tried to perfect my technique, and left the rest to the coaches.'

The pair's dedication to training was imperative to the success that they were having. Three months before a major regatta both Jumbo and Lewis would follow a strict regimen. This is taken from Jumbo's notes of 1932:

07.15	Out of bed. Glass of milk and biscuit. Training run, etc.
13.00	Lunch. Fish plainly cooked without sauce, sole, whiting etc. Salmon is not allowed.
16.15	Cup of tea and a biscuit.
22.15	Bed
Note:	No smoking. No eating or drinking between meals. Alcohol limited to half a pint of beer with lunch, 1 pint with dinner, followed by a small glass of port.

In addition to this Spartan lifestyle, Jumbo emphasised that, 'Lewis Clive and I never attended any end of term parties or Commemoration Balls. With London Rowing Club we had one hour's rest in bed after lunch. We were never permitted to go into the enclosure at Henley to watch other races because it was too off-putting, as was making polite conversation to young ladies. If any member of the crew were to break training, not only would it affect his own performance, it would affect the morals of the rest.'

Lewis had what was often described as an upper-class background. The Clive family were part of the 'Old Establishment' and whilst at Christ Church, Lewis was invited to join the exclusive and infamous Bullingdon Club. Royalty and nobility have often provided the backbone of the membership. The fame, or rather infamy, of the Bullingdon Club reached across the Atlantic. *The New York Times* informed its readers in 1913 that, 'The Bullingdon represents the acme of exclusiveness at Oxford; it is the club of the sons of nobility, the sons of great wealth; its membership represents the 'young bloods' of the university'. The newspaper went on to report that it was better known for the bad behaviour of its members, including vandalism of restaurants and students' rooms. In 1927 – two years before Lewis arrived at Christ Church – the newspapers were reporting on a night of 'high spirits'. After the Bullingdon Club dinner, members returned to Christ Church armed with hockey sticks, copper kettles, pieces of coal, and other weapons and bombarded the windows and electric globes in the famous Peckwater Quad. More than five hundred panes of glass were shattered.

With this background, it would be perfectly feasible to expect Lewis to graduate from his law degree with a political leaning that extended to the right and the Conservative Party – following the footsteps of his Conservative MP father and ancestors. Instead, Lewis would follow a different path.

In June 1932, Jumbo was continuing to hone his skills flying in his Avro. Perhaps influenced by this burning passion of his friend, or the thrill of being taken up in Jumbo's plane, Lewis accompanied Jumbo to the Oxford University Flying Squad camp to explore whether he would also be suited for a flying career. The Aeronautical Correspondent of *The Times*, in an article headlined 'Teaching Oxford Blues to Fly', gave readers an update of the camp:

> 'H. R. A. Edwards has been described as the best oar in England, and he is making so good a pilot that he will probably be given a permanent commission in the RAF. L. Clive who partnered him at

Henley when in the Pairs they won the Silver Goblets, has made good progress, and was unfortunate to lose his flying in this camp on account of measles'.

Lewis would abandon his thoughts of a career in the RAF, and instead secured a job in arguably the more mundane career of banking.

Any thoughts that the pair had on their future careers were put to one side. After the announcement of the Olympic team on July 5th, Jumbo and Lewis had just two weeks to prepare before they were to board the *Empress of Britain* at Southampton and set sail for North America.

At a time like this, one would expect an Olympic athlete to rest and relax before the arduous twelve-day journey on sea and over land to California. Jumbo, though, had other plans.

He was preparing to participate in one of the most daring and dangerous races of the sporting calendar – The King's Cup Air Race.

Chapter 9

Henley of the Skies

With only a couple of weeks of preparation before the Olympic team were due to depart, it was advised by Lord Burghley – the hurdler and captain of the Great Britain team – that all athletes should take this time to train and try to minimise any risk of injury. This was not advice that Jumbo took to heart. His love of flying was absolute, and he had already entered to compete in the annual King's Cup Race. To hell with taking life easy, Jumbo was going to race his aeroplane above the English countryside.

The King's Cup was, and remains, an annual British handicapped cross-country air race. It was first competed for in 1922 and established by King George V as an incentive to the development of light aircraft and engine design. It was the 'Henley of the skies', a chance for British (and British Empire) pilots to race against one another for the ultimate prize – a magnificent silver trophy donated by the King.

The King's Cup attracted the rich, the famous, the daring, the pioneers. Aviators such as Geoffrey de Havilland, Alex Henshaw, Nick Compton regularly competed. They were joined by famous female aviators such as Lady Mary Bailey, Winifred Brown and Winifred Spooner. The thrill of the race was too much for Jumbo and his brother Cecil to resist.

Having spent less than three years flying, Jumbo's competitive spirit wanted to rise up into the sky. He would be swapping the smooth splash of a blade entering the water with the deafening mechanical roar of his Avro engine.

Remarkably, just five days after victory in the Silver Goblets at Henley, and a mere twelve days before he was due to cross the Atlantic, Jumbo was preparing to take off from Brooklands Airfield to race against forty-one other aviators. The finest pilots in the British Empire were determined to win the prestigious trophy and, as with Henley, the races made the front pages of the newspapers.

The aeronautical historian Terry Mace describes the King's Cup as the premier air race of Britain. 'The aeroplanes (remember that the race started in 1922) were, to begin with, G-E-registered stringbags, barely able to stagger off the ground, let alone do 800-plus miles round Britain; only half of them actually finished the first race. Then the ubiquitous de Havilland Moth swept all before it for a few years but, by the mid-1930s, the race was regularly being won by the new breed of racing aeroplanes like the Percival Gull, eventually averaging well over 200 mph.'

Many of the aviators that Jumbo was to compete against had been pilots in the First World War, developing their flying skills above the battlefields of France. It truly was a case of those magnificent men – and women – in their flying machines.

On the morning of July 8th, the aeroplanes lined up at Brooklands Aerodrome. As *A Fleeting Peace* so expertly recounts, amongst the famous – and far more experienced – aviators who would race against Jumbo were Captain Hubert Broad MBE AFC, a pilot who had miraculously survived being shot through the neck in the First World War by one of Baron von Richthofen's Flying Circus pilots.

Winifred Brown was the first woman to win the King's Cup in 1930. She became an instant star across the world and especially in her home city of Salford. It was said that she learnt to roll her own cigarettes at the age of five; expelled from school at fourteen (for writing 'the headmistress can go to hell' on the toilet wall), Winifred made her first flight in 1919 from Blackpool sands.

Geoffrey de Havilland, the son of his illustrious father Sir Geoffrey de Havilland, and chief test pilot.

Flight Lieutenant Edward 'Mouse' Fielden, the pilot for the Prince of Wales (Edward VIII) and later Captain of the King's – and then the Queen's – Flights until 1962.

Captain Frederick Edward Guest, Conservative MP for Plymouth Drake, bronze medallist in polo at the 1924 Olympic Games, cousin of Winston Churchill and Secretary of State for Air in 1920–22. This Government posting was despite the fact that he knew 'very little about aviation, but it is to his credit that he does not pretend to know'.

Walter Laurence 'Wally' Hope, the two-time King's Cup winner – in 1927 and 1928. At the end of the 1928 race, C. G. Grey, one of the judges, recounted that '...thinking all was over he proceeded to loop and stunt before landing, and having landed switched on his well known winning smile. Suddenly there was a terrific hooting, and Sir Francis McClean in his white Rolls-Royce came tearing across to tell Hope he had not crossed the finishing line... Within thirty seconds Hope was in the air again, discovered the finishing line, landed, and again switched on the winning smile fortissimo.'

Angus Irwin, another First World War pilot who had been shot in the foot by Baron von Richthofen's Flying Circus pilots but had lived to tell the tale.

Caspar John – son of the famous artist and pacifist, Augustus – who would go on to be First Sea Lord and Admiral of the Fleet.

Captain Edgar Percival, the famed Australian aeronautical pioneer who designed, and piloted, some of the finest racing and record-breaking aeroplanes of all time. Michael Madigan wrote: 'It was very difficult to resist his puckish humour and not to fall under his spell... In his early flying days he had a fox-terrier called Ginger Mick. This dog always sat in

Water's Gleaming Gold

Cecil's Blackburn Bluebird IV on the airfield before the start of the King's Cup Air Race, 1931.

the [open] rear cockpit tethered to a spar. One day as Edgar was preparing to land he went into a loop to lose height, forgetting about his four-legged passenger. After levelling off he heard strange scrabbling noises from the back and looking out saw Ginger Mick frantically dog-paddling in the air suspended by his lead. Edgar managed to manoeuvre Ginger back into the plane, and after landing he thought he would never see Ginger Mick again as he rushed off. However, Ginger was as persistent an aviator as his master and reappeared to settle back into his passenger seat at start-up, large as life, and eager for more.'

Squadron Leader John Woodhouse, a well-known car and motorcycle racer. In the First World War he was the first pilot to land a spy successfully behind the German lines. Later in the war he was also lost over the North Sea for several hours after having attacked and driven off a Zeppelin.

This was just a few of the forty-one personalities that were about to start their engines and roar off into the Surrey skies above the aerodrome.

There were two other competitors that Jumbo knew very well and who he would have to compete against. The first of these was the reigning King's Cup holder, his brother Sphinx. Cecil had achieved national fame the previous year by winning the King's Cup.

Oliver Stewart of *The Tatler* reported on Sphinx's victory in 1931.

> Since 1925, when it was flown in dense fog, I do not remember a King's Cup flown in worse weather. Torrential rain, low clouds, and a variable wind prevailed over all but two sections of the 982 ½ miles' course. At Heston the weather conditions were appalling, but they were rightly not allowed to interrupt the pageant programme though they interfered with the enjoyment of the Duke and Duch-

ess of York and other spectators. In view of the weather the greater must be the credit accorded to the winner, Flying Officer E. C. T. Edwards and to his Blackburn 'Bluebird' Mark IV for averaging nearly 118 mph, the highest speed at which any 'light' aeroplane has won the event.

Jumbo was at Heston Aerodrome to proudly witness his brother accepting the King's Cup from Sir Philip Sassoon, Under-Secretary of State for Air, in front of a cheering crowd. The photograph would be splashed on the front page of newspapers, and his victory shown on Pathé News in all the cinemas.

As Jumbo recounted, 'Robert MacAlpine, the wealthy Scottish construction millionaire, had loaned Sphinx for the race a Blackburn Bluebird – a two-seater side-by-side named 'King Cobra'. He had the assistance of Corporal Heighley, a brilliant craftsman. Sphinx explained that he was unable to afford to pay him for his help, but if he won any monetary award he would share it. The basic Bluebird was a very slow aeroplane but they reviewed and examined everything from the exhaust stubs to the smallest fitting and nut. They rebuilt the enormous cockpit and beat out new engine cowling panels. All these improvements had to be declared on the race entry form, and were duly checked by the handicappers, Messrs Dancy and Howarth. The race was right around England and Wales, starting and finishing at Heston. The weather turned very nasty in the afternoon with low clouds and rain, but a few minutes earlier than expected, in a roar from the west, a Bluebird appeared just over the aerodrome buildings and flashed across the finishing line minutes ahead of any other competitor. Sphinx had done it! We ran across the grass field to greet him.'

For Sphinx it was a day that he would never forget. After losing three Boat Races he had finally won one of sport's most coveted trophies.

Interviewed shortly after clambering out of his Bluebird, Sphinx breathlessly recounted the race to a reporter: 'It was pretty hard going at times.

Water's Gleaming Gold

Left: A victorious Sphinx climbs down from his plane after winning the King's Cup. Right: Sir Philip Sassoon hands over the trophy, which would soon be in the clutches of Sir Robert MacAlpine.

The visibility was not more than a hundred yards. I had quite a big handicap to get over, but Mr MacAlpine's plane stood me in good stead. I felt sure after I had left Bristol that I had overtaken Flight Lieutenant Gibbons, although in the bad visibility I never once saw him during those last exciting minutes, I knew it was neck or nothing, and went all out. It was when I saw the crowd waving their hands and running towards me that I realised I had won the Cup. It was a wonderful moment – a moment I shall never forget. I am, of course, proud of my victory.'

Later that day an exhausted Sphinx was invited to Sir Robert MacAlpine's palatial Sussex home to celebrate the victory. Sir Robert asked Sphinx to bring with him the magnificent trophy that was awarded to the victorious pilot. When it was time for an exhausted Sphinx to make his excuses and leave the celebrations, Sir Robert gave him a cheery 'Well done Edwards', grabbed the trophy and that was the last time Sphinx or the Edwards family saw it. In 2006 the trophy did re-appear, mysteriously donated by a Vincent Saunders to Henley Regatta where it is now renamed as The Prince of Wales Challenge Cup and awarded to the winning men's quadruple sculls crew.

This year, Jumbo would have to compete against his brother. The other aviator that Jumbo and – especially – Sphinx were more than familiar with was Winifred Spooner.

'Bad luck Wimpey' was one of the best-known women aviators of the time, and the one generally regarded as the most talented. Winifred was awarded the International League of Aviation's Trophy for women aviators in 1929, and a year later Captain C. D. Barnard described her as 'the finest woman pilot in the world'. Having learnt to fly in 1926, Winifred won her first race in April 1928 at the age of twenty-six – the Suffolk Handicap – ahead of Neville Stack and four other male rivals. In the King's Cup she had finished a creditable third in 1928, and fifth in both 1929 and 1931.

Winifred was not only an extremely talented aviator but she was a regular feature in the national press, and *Good Housekeeping* employed her to write articles on 'Flying for Women'. Having competed against Sphinx in air races over the past few years, the two had formed a firm friendship. In December 1930 they made a daring decision – to prove to the world that an aeroplane could fly from London to Cape Town within five days, setting a new record.

On the early morning of December 5th, reporters gathered at a bitterly cold Croydon Aerodrome to witness Winifred and Sphinx embark on their six thousand mile journey south

> 'Just before daybreak today a small DeSouttar monoplane roared away into the darkness from Croydon aerodrome. Its occupants were Miss Winifred Spooner, the famous airwoman, and Flying Officer E. C. T. Edwards. Their destination, Cape Town. It was bitterly cold when the machine took off from the brilliantly lighted landing ground today, and next Sunday, after long distance hops over the sea and tropical forests, the flyers will, if all goes well, be enjoying the warmth of a South African winter'. (*Liverpool Echo*)

A few minutes before she climbed up into the cockpit Miss Spooner explained to a reporter that her object was to demonstrate that the Imperial Airways Service, which was shortly to be started from London to Cape Town, could be accomplished in five days.

Winifred Spooner (second from left) and Cecil (far right) photographed before their early morning departure to Cape Town, 1930.

'By day and night flying,' Winifred declared, 'it is possible on paper to get to the Cape in that time. We hope to prove that it is possible in practice. Flying Officer Edwards and myself will take turns to pilot the machine and while one is in charge the other will be sleeping. Our first stop will be Rome, which city we hope to reach tonight. Then we shall fly on to Benghazi, then to Khartoum, and so by the usual route to the Cape.'

Winifred flashed a beaming smile and shouted down, 'The weather this morning is perfect for flying. And now we'll be off.'

Winifred and Sphinx made good time on that December day. They flew south over the Channel then landed briefly at airstrips in France to refuel. They made it to Rome on schedule in the early evening. After another brief stop to refuel and to have a light supper, Sphinx took to the controls and the Desoutter continued its journey down the Italian coast.

Sixteen hours after they had departed Croydon the Desoutter was flying over the Tyrrenhian sea, a few miles off the Calabrian coast of southern Italy. Winifred was catching up with some sleep and the weather had deteriorated, with rain and a strong wind buffeting the aeroplane as Sphinx struggled with the controls.

What happened next has always been shrouded in mystery – with the Press all reporting different stories. But the recollection of Sphinx was that, 'whilst I was flying the aircraft and while Winifred was asleep, the plane crashed into the sea off the coast of Belmonte Calabro in complete darkness. I cannot give a reason for the plane steadily losing height without my knowledge. I was injured and Winifred left me sitting on the wooden fuselage and volunteered to swim the two miles ashore six strokes at a time. She then alerted local fishermen, who rescued me and the plane.'

The *Daily Mirror* published the daring escapade of Sphinx and Winifred on their front page, but had utilised some rather inventive reporting on the facts. The article was headlined with 'British Girl Flyer Thrown from 'Plane into Sea – 240ft Fall and a Swim for Life'. The reader was thrilled with, 'An amazing story of her ordeal… blown from her aeroplane during a storm and fell 240ft into the sea'.

As for Sphinx, he was misquoted in stating that 'I called for help for four hours and believed my end had come. I took a sheet of paper, writing a few words to put into the bottle. After ten hours a boat arrived with Miss Spooner and I was rescued'. It was all highly exaggerated.

Winifred and Sphinx recuperated in Italy under the care and supervision of the locals and the Italian Air Minister, General Balbo, who had befriended Winifred during an air race in Venice the previous year. General Balbo sent a telegram to England and Lord Amulree, Secretary of State for Air, giving details of the accident and reassuring that: 'The two sufferers are enjoying cordial hospitality of the Mayor of Belmonte and surrounded by every care. Aircraft is on beach awaiting dismantling. Acting on my instructions, an officer left Naples air station by air at dawn this morning to place himself at disposal of pilots for anything they may require.'

Winifred arrived back in England on December 22nd, and was greeted at Victoria Station by hundreds of schoolgirls who had revelled in the stories of her adventures. She immediately spoke to the Press and refuted the 'preposterous stories' that had been spread about the ditching.

'How could I fly in an aeroplane at 100 miles an hour, be flung out 200 feet into the sea, and then get up and swim? I should not feel much like swimming, and neither would anyone else. Everyone who knows anything about aeroplanes will be roaring with laughter at some of the tales about me. And how would I fall out of an aeroplane? Simply to get out of the thing is difficult enough, goodness knows. Yes, it is true though that I did have to swim for two hours in the sea.'

Winifred returned to her home town of Wokingham and in recognition of her epic swim the Mayor and Corporation of Wokingham gave her a Civic Reception. She was driven to the Town Hall on a fire engine that struggled to make it through the cheering crowds.

The previous day, Sphinx arrived back home having flown into Hendon Aerodrome. There were no school children to greet his arrival. He travelled back to his mother's home in West London to tell his relieved family the story of his lucky escape from the floating debris of their aeroplane.

Jumbo was certainly not lacking in flying practice or participating in competitions, but he definitely lacked his brother's experience. By the middle of 1931, 'I had put in about two hundred and fifty hours of flying on about a dozen different types of aircraft and I began to think of myself as quite a good pilot, an opinion which was enhanced when I was selected to join the team of three to represent Oxford in the air race against Cambridge held at Duxford. Flying a Gipsy Moth I won the first heat and then the final. At that meeting there was an air display and one of the events was an acrobatic show by an Avro Avian. The pilot was diving down to gain speed before carrying out an upward roll when the starboard lower wing broke up and he dived, fatally, straight into the deck.'

The dangers of flying were all too apparent, and death was a constant threat.

Hugh standing proudly beside his Avro Baby aeroplane, 1930.

On the morning of Friday, July 8th, the forty-two aviators prepared their planes for the start of the King's Cup. Jumbo was given the starting number of 18, and was flying a single seat 'sports plane' – a Southern Martlet (only six were ever built). This was Sphinx's own aeroplane. Sphinx had been lent an Arrow Active I, declining any offer of an aeroplane from Sir Robert MacAlpine. The Arrow Active was also a single seat biplane but was built primarily as an acrobatic plane.

The route for Day One of the race was to take the aviators from Brooklands Aerodrome in Surrey south west to Portsmouth and then due north as far as Liverpool, due south east to Ipswich and then back to Brooklands – covering seven hundred and thirty-eight miles.

Jumbo had flown Sphinx's Martlet before and had meticulously planned for the operation of the manual fuel pump. 'I had attended to every little detail, even to writing on my strip maps at appropriate intervals the word "PUMP".'

Jumbo was progressing well, pushing his aeroplane to the limit and keeping his flying height to a minimum to avoid any air turbulence. He had flown over Liverpool and was heading due east to Manchester when, at five hundred feet, the engine cut out. 'I had overlooked my executive instruction to Pump.'

The aeroplane went into a steeply banked turn. In that fleeting moment Jumbo realised that any plans of packing his kitbag for the trip to the Olympics were now in the balance. His plane was hurtling downwards and towards a field outside of Warrington. He should be at home relaxing, going for a gentle row along the Thames, trying out his tailored Great Britain blazer and Panama hat.

'I had not quite enough height or speed to complete the banked turn that the empty fuel tank had given me. But the Martlet was a splendid aeroplane. I landed perfectly, but at an angle, and collided with the hedge, giving it a glancing blow which did not do the starboard wing much good. So I was out of the race and ingloriously had to have her dismantled and loaded in to a lorry for return to the south.'

This was the end of Jumbo's King's Cup. Sphinx would go on to compete in the remaining stages and finished tenth, with Winifred fifteenth. The winner was Walter 'Wally' Hope, his third victory in the competition.

Out of the forty-two competitors, thirty-one went on to finish the race. Tragically, over a third of all those who competed in that year's King's Cup never lived past the year 1945. Several were killed whilst serving for the RAF, in flying accidents during aircraft tests or competing in air races.

Winifred Spooner was one who died too young. Just a few months after the King's Cup, in January 1933, Winifred succumbed to a very short illness. As reported in *The Times*,

> 'Miss Winifred Spooner, the famous airwoman, died last night at her home at Ratcliffe Aerodrome, Leicester. She had been ill only a day. The symptoms were those of influenza, but her condition gave no cause for alarm until the evening. She became worse, and a specialist hurried from Nottingham by motor-car, but Miss Spooner died in two hours... her loss will be felt by aviation as a whole. She had no desire for publicity and was rarely tempted to undertake big

flights for the sake of the notice they would win her. She talked with the greatest reserve of what she did. Her success as a professional pilot is probably one of the soundest pieces of aviation propaganda which any woman has done.'

In 1936, the Winifred Spooner Memorial Prize was founded at her former school, Sherborne Girls' School. This prize was to be awarded annually to a pupil demonstrating 'courage, enterprise, independence and generosity of mind'. A fitting memorial for such a pioneering woman and aviator.

At her funeral at Hinton Parva, a small village near Swindon, all the residents turned out to pay their respects. The villagers were joined by the most illustrious names in aviation. There was a carpet of flowers, prominent among them a magnificent wreath from General Balbo.

As the congregation filed out of the churchyard one mourner detached himself from the crowd and walked back to the bright garland of flowers.

Beside the Italian wreath, in the falling snow, Sphinx stood silently by Winifred's grave.

Chapter 10

The Promised Land

Jumbo returned to London after his mishap in the Warrington field. His crash landing had made the national papers and he was half expecting a very strongly worded letter of rebuke from Lord Burghley, the captain of the Olympic team. But none arrived.

Lewis Clive was understandably far from amused but he had as much faith in Jumbo's ability to land a stricken aircraft as he had in his skill to row down a straight course of water. Five days after he had crashed out of the King's Cup, on Wednesday, July 13th, the *Empress of Britain* was to set sail from Southampton bound for Quebec. From Quebec, it would be a long and gruelling journey by train to Los Angeles and the Opening Ceremony on Friday, July 29th.

King George V sent a message of encouragement to the team:

> 'As patron of the British Olympic Association I send you all my best wishes for success in the Olympic Games. Know that whatever the results may be you will display that pluck and good sportsmanship so traditional of the British race. I shall follow your contests with the greatest interest, fully confident that you will maintain a spirit of good and comradeship amongst your fellow competitors'.

On the Wednesday morning, seventy-two British athletes arrived at Waterloo to take the train down to Southampton – a second, smaller, contingent were to depart two days later. They were met by a vast cheering crowd waving Union Jack flags.

Jumbo's lack of preparation for the journey was made apparent to his sister Mona on the evening before the departure: she had to spend the whole night hand-washing his dirty rowing kit, mangling it and then ironing the kit dry. Handing over the pile of clean laundry in the morning, Jumbo then admitted that he had no money for the whole trip. As Jumbo made his way to Waterloo, Mona rushed to her bank in the Strand, waited impatiently until it opened, withdrew her whole balance and then rushed to Waterloo to hand over the money in time for Jumbo to board the train to the *Empress of Britain*. She made it with minutes to spare.

Jumbo was taken aback by the sheer size of the welcoming crowd, but soon realised that they were excitedly thronging around a different delegation to the one that he was in. The train – and subsequently the *Empress of Britain* – was transporting a Government delegation to the British Empire Economic Conference in Ottawa. With an inevitable realisation, Jumbo spotted his nemesis from so many racing regattas – the former Prime Minister Stanley Baldwin.

The Government delegation also included Neville Chamberlain (Chancellor of the Exchequer), Viscount Hailsham (Secretary of State for War), Sir Philip Cunliffe-Lister (Secretary of State for the Colonies) and other dignitaries and industrialists. The world was in the midst of the Great Depression and the Conference was intended to address economic reform within the British Empire. The principle was to be 'home producers first, Empire producers second, and foreign producers last'. The crowds who had flocked to Waterloo station held a great hope in their politicians. It was an optimism that the Government delegation could provide a salvation from the economic woes that had so destabilised the country.

'The British nation has built great hopes on the Ottawa Conference. The grievous problems which afflict the world today cannot be solved by the application of the old remedies: they demand totally new methods of approach and the use of scientific fact and thought. When all is approaching chaos it is for Britain to initiate the recovery, a task which alone may well be too much for the nation, but with the aid of our far-flung Empire the possibilities of success will be infinitely greater.' (*The Times*)

As Jumbo and the rest of the Olympic team boarded the train, Stanley Baldwin – resplendent in a summer suit – addressed the throngs.

'We are leaving full of hope that we shall be able, as a further step towards the revival of the trade of the world, to crown the first year's work of the National Government by agreeing at Ottawa upon a policy of freer trade, which will lay the foundation of a great expansion of Empire trade, to the mutual advantage of us all. We look to the people at home to play their part in the task of national restoration by giving overwhelming support, thus helping our industries on the path of recovery and strengthening Great Britain's position in the eyes of the whole world.'

The ocean liner *Empress of Britain*, dubbed the '*Empress of Hope*' by the Press, was waiting at Southampton docks for the athletes and politicians. Sir Harry Bowden, Chairman of the British Olympic Committee (BOC), had overseen the raising of public funds to ensure that Great Britain could send a team to Los Angeles. A total of £10,000 – equivalent to just under £1 million today – was contributed by the British public to allow the athletes to travel.

The Great Depression coupled with the vast amount of miles required to travel to California, had challenged many countries in sending a team. This resulted in a drastically reduced travelling party. At the 1928 Olympics, Great Britain had assembled two hundred and thirty-two athletes for the short trip across the North Sea to Amsterdam. In 1932, there were less than half this number of competitors and this was entirely due to the cost of sending a team six thousand miles across the globe and back again.

As late as September 1931, Sweden proposed the cancellation of the

1932 Games because of the economic woes of the Great Depression; many European countries, including Germany and France, were struggling to raise the necessary funds to send a team and agreed with their Swedish counterparts. Six months before the Games were to open the American President, Herbert Hoover, informed organisers he would not be attending due to pressing economic issues in the capital. The President did not want to be associated with California's frivolous 'athletic carnival'. Vice President Charles Curtis would be sent instead.

In 1931 when Bowden was appointed Chairman of the BOC, he reiterated the policy that due to the 'depressed state of industry, and the high costs of transporting a team to California, only competitors who had a real chance of a place in the final of their event, and officials who were absolutely essential, could be assisted in going to the Olympics'. The prospect of a reduction in team size compared with previous Olympics was accompanied by a scaling down of medal aspirations.

Despite the restrictions to the team, there remained a hope that medals were to be won in California. Bowden happily addressed the Press on the gangplank: 'I am proud to be commandant of this team. We have a grand team, the best this country can produce under the handicap of inadequate funds. And we shall not let the Old Country down.'

With those rousing words the *Empress of Britain* set sail.

The athletes were given berths in the 'Tourist Class' section of the liner; the politicians and industrialists were afforded the more spacious and luxurious Second and First Class cabins. The newspapers were incredulous that the hurdler and captain of the team, Lord Burghley, had insisted on travelling under exactly the same conditions as the rest of the team. Lord Burghley proudly declared, 'Since the British effort has had to be financed wholly by private subscription, it has been essential to exercise the strictest economy in all the arrangements. There should not be any preferential treatment for any of the athletes.'

The conditions on board the *Empress of Britain* – even within Tourist Class – still induced a feeling of wonder in Jumbo. In a letter written on

On the deck of the Empress of Britain. *From left-to-right: Hugh, Jack Beresford, Tom Askwith and Thomas Tyler,* © *Jack Beresford's Family.*

his arrival in Los Angeles to his sister Mona, Jumbo describes the five-day voyage to Quebec.

'We had a very pleasant trip out here and although we travelled tourist class, we more or less had the run of the whole boat and used the swimming bath etc. as much as we liked. There was plenty to do all day – tennis, deck-tennis, squash, cinema and dancing.'

The athletes had a programme of fitness to also adhere to, and would run circuits around the liner – Jumbo always determined to avoid any unnecessary contact with Stanley Baldwin.

With all of the activities, the Atlantic crossing went quickly. It remained uneventful until the liner reached the coast of Canada.

'We should probably have broken the speed record for the trip if we had not run into fog off Newfoundland. Just off St Lawrence we collided with a steamer in a thick fog, but we didn't sustain much damage. As the other boat faded away into the fog, we saw the crew very busy getting the lifeboats out and our hope was that they all got safely away.'

The *Empress of Britain* was met by a loud and celebratory Canadian crowd. As with their departure from Waterloo train station, Jumbo soon discovered that the crowd was there to enthusiastically welcome the politicians.

The athletes and politicians – the collective bearers of political and sporting hope for Great Britain – said their farewells and departed for their respective destinations. For the politicians, they boarded a train bound for Ottawa. For Jumbo and his fellow athletes it was a train to Toronto and, grudgingly for the rowers, a stay of three days 'for the benefit of the runners'.

The Great Britain Olympic team are met in Chicago by Mary Pickford and Douglas Fairbanks in their gleaming white automobile
© *Jack Beresford's Family.*

The crews unpacked the boats and did some rowing on Lake Ontario to resharpen their oarsmanship that had rusted up from the long ocean voyage.

The last time that Jumbo had been flying was on the ill-fated stage of the King's Cup, but with a letter of introduction from his aviator friend and rival – Geoffrey de Havilland – Jumbo escaped from the hotel. He jumped into a taxi and headed to the de Havilland Aerodrome in downtown Toronto. In his letter home he simply wrote, 'I did a little flying'.

After three days of training in Canada, it was time for the Great Britain team to head across the border and westwards to Los Angeles.

The first stop on the rail journey to the Xth Olympiad: Chicago.

Chicago was still in the grip of prohibition. Although Al Capone had been imprisoned on tax evasion charges a couple of months earlier, for Jumbo and his fellow rowers it was in their imagination an intoxicating city of notorious gangsters and bootleg booze. In the letter to Mona, Jumbo wrote – rather disappointedly – 'We didn't see any murders at all'.

When the team arrived in Chicago, they were greeted by 'America's Sweetheart' – the movie star Mary Pickford – in her gleaming white car. This enticing glance of Hollywood glamour was short-lived – they only

The Promised Land

had a half day in Chicago before they had to embark on the Santa Fe railway for Los Angeles. The only scheduled 'long stop for exercise' would be at Albuquerque. As Jumbo described to Mona, 'The train journey from Chicago was rather unpleasant. It was frightfully hot and most of the country was desert'.

The stop at Albuquerque allowed them all to stretch their legs and begin to acclimatise to the heat of an American summer. Jumbo acquired a pair of moccasins from some enterprising Native Americans; they assured him that they would bring him good luck.

At midday on Monday, July 25th, the athletes arrived in Los Angeles. This was the culmination of a twelve-day odyssey from the bustle and greyness of Waterloo station to the blazing sunshine of the City of Angels.

Los Angeles in the early 1930s was 'the Promised Land that amazes, delights and will thaw you out physically and spiritually; an open-air circus of mixed cultures that includes educational, scientific, industrial, and

Hugh poses on the front of the locomotive that would transport the Great Britain team from Chicago to Los Angeles and the Xth Olympic Games © Jack Beresford's Family.

entertainment characteristics'. However, the Great Depression and the consequent limitations for competing nations to send large delegations of athletes had led to a pessimism about the Games within California and the world at large. Bill Henry, the technical director for the Games wrote:

> 'In the spring of 1932, it was the freely expressed opinion of disinterested observers that the Games either would not be held at all or, if held, would be a farce. And then, almost overnight, the whole atmosphere changed. The arrival of teams in their colorful uniforms in New York and other ports electrified sports lovers; newspapers turned their pages over to this startling development; those who had bought their season tickets a year previous to the Games and had the choice locations in the great stadium became the envy of their friends; people started for Los Angeles by train, steamer, motor, airplane, as the word spread.'

Through nationwide promotion and the creation of the very first Olympic village, the organisers produced a blueprint that was followed by Olympiads for the rest of the 20th Century. In trumpeting the arrival of the Olympic Games, the organisers decreed that the Xth Olympic Games would be a 'modern cultural event'. This cultural celebration would include the world's greatest amateur athletes, a chance to rub elbows with celebrities, explore Spanish mission ruins, and experience the Mediterranean-like climate of ancient Greece in Southern California.

People flocked to Los Angeles.

The creation of a dedicated Olympic Village for the athletes was an important factor in the decision to award Los Angeles the Games. Previous to 1932, athletes and a nation's contingent of officials had to find their own accommodation. During the 1912 Games in Stockholm – and again in 1928, in Amsterdam – athletes and coaches from the United States trained and slept on the liner that had brought them across the Atlantic.

Located in Baldwin Hills in southern Los Angeles, the Olympic Village comprised over five hundred portable houses. The complex also included a post office, cinema, hospital, bank and a range of other amenities. The Official Report of the Games, dripping with Olympian imagery, described the Village as 'a miniature city, replete with modern conveniences and facilities, arisen magically atop the hills within eyesight of the great Olympic Stadium – atop the modern Mount Olympus, below which lie the modern plains of Elis'.

Jumbo was definitely impressed, 'The village is a dream of a place. Four athletes live in each bungalow.'

The Great Britain team was transported swiftly to the Village to be allocated their bungalows. The women, however, were not part of this contingent. All of the female athletes were instead ushered to the downtown Chapman Park Hotel – the prospect of young, athletic male and female competitors mixing and socialising together was just too dangerous for the organisers to allow.

Each sporting discipline within the Great Britain team had a manager – and the rowers had been appointed the 52-year-old George Drinkwater. George, as with Jumbo, had attended Dragon School in Oxford and had gained his Blue by competing for Oxford in the Boat Races of 1902 and 1903. He was also a renowned artist, author and the rowing correspondent for *The Daily Telegraph*. George wanted to ensure all fifteen of his rowers had the very best of living conditions to go alongside their training. The rowers' delight with the Village surroundings and with the mingling of all the international athletes was to come to a premature end.

'We stayed one night at the Olympic Village and then went out to Long Beach for our first practice on the course. However, George decided that it was too long a run to do daily, it was over twenty miles to the course, and fixed up accommodation for us at the Robinson Hotel at Long Beach. So we packed our bags and left the Village.'

The Long Beach Marine Stadium was one of the few sporting locations that was built specifically for the Games. A thorough survey of water courses adjacent to Los Angeles found none able to meet Olympic rowing requirements. A lagoon in Long Beach was merited as promising, except for being approximately five hundred metres too short. The City of Long Beach and the Los Angeles Olympic Organising Committee (LAOOC) entered into an agreement in which the City agreed to dredge the lagoon to the necessary length and depth. The LAOOC agreed to finance the construction of grandstands, a boat house, docks, starting platforms and buildings for dressing rooms.

The Long Beach course was officially opened on July 23rd, just two days prior to the arrival of the British team. An estimated 120,000 spectators flocked to watch the dress-rehearsal for the big event. Those lucky enough to have access to the grandstands watched enthralled as the height of the stadium allowed them to watch the races from the start to the finish post.

The British rowers were impressed with the course.

'The course of two thousand metres was cut from a lagoon connected with the sea', Jumbo recalled. 'One didn't notice any appreciable rise and fall of the tide, nor, indeed, that the water was salt. The western side of the course was dotted with oil rigs working away.'

Jumbo and his teammates settled into the hotel. The training routine was – in Jumbo's word – 'normal', with a 'morning outing at 10.30 a.m. in the still air with the sun shining out of a blue sky. At 11.15 a.m. a sea breeze would begin to blow and this made conditions very pleasant. The four with experienced men like Jack Beresford and Felix Badcock coached themselves on Fairbairn lines as Lewis and I did in our pair. The eight was coached on orthodox lines by George Drinkwater. The second outing would be in the cool of the late afternoon.'

With the team now acclimated to the Californian summer, the day of the Opening Ceremony had arrived. In Jumbo's letter home to Mona, dated on the morning of July 30th, he wrote: 'The Games open this afternoon with a procession round the arena by all the athletes. I hope they will get the ceremony over quickly and not keep us standing in the sun too long.'

The Opening Ceremony was to be held in the Olympic Stadium – later renamed the Los Angeles Memorial Coliseum. Commissioned in 1921 and completed two years later, the stadium's capacity had been increased to over 105,000 for the Games. Standing thirty-two metres high, its signature torch-shaped Olympic cauldron was installed atop the central arch of the peristyle and housed the Olympic flame that would burn throughout the two weeks of competition. It was a magnificent sight for the athletes.

At 2.30 p.m. the British athletes lined up in the depths of the stadium. Lord Burghley, holding the Union Jack aloft, was ready to lead his team out of the darkness and into the glaring afternoon sunshine. Although the British team was reduced in numbers, one hundred and eight competitors had travelled and were now ready to parade out into the sunshine. The British Press were confident despite the limited size of the contingent.

> 'Lord Burghley, sportsman, democrat and diplomat, will carry the Union Jack at the head of Great Britain's small and brilliant team. It must be agreed that in numerical strength our team at Los Angeles does not compare with Antwerp, Paris, or Amsterdam, but the necessary cutting down of numbers may be a blessing in disguise inasmuch as athletes have had to show exceptional form to gain recognition'. (*The Times*)

The Organising Committee had spared no effort to ensure the perfection of every detail to ensure a magnificent pageant. In the stadium were seated 3,500 professional musicians – 1,200 choristers, 1,500 band members and 800 members of the drum and bugle corps. It was by far the greatest attendance ever at an Olympic Opening Ceremony, with 105,000 people eagerly awaiting the entrance of the teams and the lighting of the flame.

Whilst waiting for their entry, Jumbo could hear the Star-Spangled Banner sung by the 3,500 musicians in the chorus. The last sung note was the cue for the athletes to march out and enter the great bowl of the athletics field. Every nation was greeted with a great roar from the crowd.

The Great Britain team were resplendent in their dark blue team blazers, white slacks and with a Panama hat to try and keep some of the sun at bay. The fifteen rowers marched together in the parade.

Along with Jumbo and Clive, as the coxless pairs, the eight were the Cambridge crew that had triumphed both in the Boat Race and in the Leander colours at Henley of that year: Tom Askwith, David Haig-Thomas, Charles Sergel, Donald McCowen, Kenneth Payne, Harold Rickett, William Sambell, Lewis Luxton and John Ranking. Sambell and Luxton had been runners-up to Jumbo and Lewis in the Silver Goblets at the 1931 Henley Regatta, and although they were both Australian, they had opted to row for Great Britain.

Due to insufficient funds, the Australian Amateur Rowing Council had selected only one rower – the supremely talented Bobby Pearce in the single sculls. Even then it took a guarantee from Bobby Pearce to the AARC that he would only compete at his own expense, as he was living in Canada. He drove the three thousand miles from Hamilton, Ontario, to Los Angeles with his boat on the roof of the car.

As Britain's representative for the single sculls, Leslie 'Dick' Southwood would go up against Pearce.

The coxless four were represented by the Thames Rowing Club quartet of Jack Beresford, John 'Felix' Badcock, Rowland George and Thomas 'Tig' Tyler.

Despite their intense rivalries at regattas, these fifteen rowers that comprised the British team had built up a friendship. A genuine comradeship had grown over the last two weeks of constant travel and training. Jumbo was especially friendly with Jack Beresford, his hero from those school days when he would watch Jack scull down the Thames. On the long train journey, Jumbo would listen attentively as Jack recounted stories of previous Olympics.

The rivalry between the rowing clubs of London and Thames were put to one side. The arduous odyssey to California was for their country, not for any individual glory.

Chapter 11

Luck of the Moccasins

With the lighting of the Olympic flame, the Games had begun. For the first time in Olympic history the events had been scheduled over sixteen days. Previous Games had gone on for several weeks or even months. This truncated format has remained in place ever since. The rowers though would have to wait ten days before the regatta commenced – it would be the last major event of the programme.

After training sessions had finished, Jumbo and his team mates would go along to the Olympic Stadium to cheer on the British contingent. They were in the stadium to watch their captain, Lord Burghley, attempt to defend his 400 metres hurdles gold medal that he had won in 1928. But there was to be no repeat victory.

> 'Lord Burghley found the pace too hot for him, and though hurdling in beautiful style, could not quite catch up higher than fourth in a great finish. Lord Burghley's great popularity here drew a prolonged and sympathetic cheer when the announcement of the placing was made' (*The Manchester Guardian*)

The team was able to celebrate British success on the track. In the final of the 800 metres, Tommy Hampson of Great Britain was placed fourth

The view from Robinson Hotel at Long Beach, where the rowing crews were staying, overlooking the Rainbow Pier © Jack Beresford's Family.

when rounding the final bend. As the runners approached the final straight, Hampson put in an electrifying burst which carried him up to the leaders. It was not until the last few desperate steps that he succeeded in getting the better of the Canadian, Alex Wilson, and only by hurling himself at the tape did Hampson win the gold. Hampson collapsed on the track, his chest heaving, trying to regain his breath. His victory was in an Olympic record time of one minute and forty-nine seconds.

A day later there was further British success. Tommy Green, at the age of thirty-eight and having suffered from the debilitating affliction of rickets as an infant, was victorious in the 50 km walk. What made the victory even more astounding was that Tommy had to stride along in heat so intense that only seven out of the fifteen competitors finished.

To further relax and try to get their minds away from the competition, the rowers would head out in the evening to Rainbow Pier outside of their hotel.

As Jumbo wrote in his letter home, 'In the evenings we sometimes go to the fair here, which is rather a good one. There is a roller coaster called the 'Cyclone Racer' which is about twice as thrilling as the one at Wembley because you rush down incredibly steep slopes, turning all the time, so that you cannot see where you are going. Also there is a sort of aeroplane mounted on gimbals, with an airscrew and controls like a real aeroplane, but it is almost uncontrollable.'

Four days before the start of the rowing heats, Thomas 'Tig' Tyler who rowed at number three in the coxless four informed George Drinkwater that he would have to miss out on the afternoon training session as he was feeling 'light headed'. The following day Tig was unable to get out of his bed – a high temperature confirmed his, and the team's, worst fears that he had contracted influenza. Tig had to be confined to his room for fear that it would afflict the others.

For these Olympic Games, Great Britain could not afford to include in the travelling contingent any reserves to replace a stricken athlete. Drinkwater was now left with a difficult decision. With Tig unable to train would he be fit enough, or even well enough, to compete in the heats? Having travelled six thousand miles, Drinkwater was about to make a decision that would be heartbreaking to the Thames rower.

The team were called to a meeting in the hotel. After consulting with Tig's fellow crew, Beresford, George and Badcock, it was decided that Jumbo would be replacing Tig in the boat. Beresford was moved to number two, and Jumbo would take up the rudder and Tig's oar at number three.

A sudden realisation dawned on Jumbo, 'I was now the only man in the whole regatta who was rowing in two events'.

Lewis was not pleased. He angrily reacted to Drinkwater's decision by arguing that his medal hopes were now at jeopardy as Jumbo would not be able to give his whole attention to their pairing. But the decision remained, and the coxless four – with Jumbo settling in beside his Thames rivals – took to the water to familiarise themselves with one another's technique. Jumbo's reaction after the first practice: 'We fitted in quite well'.

When Jumbo returned to his hotel room, he took out his Olympic programme of events to examine the schedule. A dread realisation hit home.

Young autograph hunters gather outside the team dressing rooms at Long Beach © Jack Beresford's Family.

If he was to progress through the heats, he would have to compete in two finals within less than an hour of one another. This was clearly an impossibility.

Jumbo lay back on his bed and put the schedule of races to the back of his mind. He comforted himself with the thought that Tig would be back to full health in no time. Tig would regain his position in the coxless four, if the heats could be successfully negotiated. A quick glance at the Olympic rulebook soon ruled this out: 'While there are elimination races there may not be a change made in the team which runs in the finals'. No one had yet told Tig.

The rowing programme commenced on Tuesday, August 9th, with the heats for the single and double sculls. There were seven disciplines in the 1932 regatta: single sculls, double sculls, coxless pairs, coxed pairs, coxless fours, coxed fours and the eights. Great Britain was competing in four of the events. On the Tuesday it was Dick Southwood, in the single sculls, who would begin the British quest for medals.

The team were at the Long Beach stadium to watch Dick take to the water at 9 a.m. For the first time in an Olympic regatta the width of the course allowed four crews to race abreast, eliminating the need for excessive heats, and making an exciting spectacle for the crowd. There were five entries for the single sculls, and so the two heats were in reality the semi-finals – the winner would automatically advance to the final, with the losers racing off in the repechage for the remaining two places in the final.

Dick was drawn to face the Uruguayan, Guillermo Douglas, and the Canadian, Joseph Wright Jr. Bobby Pearce, heavily fancied for gold, had been drawn in the other heat against the home favourite, William Miller. Dick won his heat easily, winning by a length from Douglas. He was through to the finals on the Saturday. Dick was joined by Bobby Pearce who disappointed the large partisan crowd by easily sending the American, Miller, to the repechage.

Dick's winning performance provided an excellent boost to the team, who were still coming to terms with Tig's confinement in the hotel.

After watching the heats, Jumbo and Lewis took a walk down the course, talking through the stroke rates and tactics. They passed by some hot dog stands. Lewis exclaimed, 'Oh Jumbo, look at those apple pies. Let's have some'. Jumbo, knowing that it would not unduly affect Lewis replied, 'Go ahead, Lewis. I'll wait'. Jumbo had been rowing for twelve years by this time and he knew perfectly well what he could and could not do with regard to food. However, as he was to admit years later, 'During the Games I had been surreptitiously smoking three cigarettes a day, but I did not let Lewis know'.

Further breaking of the strict regimen was to follow that day.

'After returning from our walk, a young American lady staying in the hotel pointed out to me that my lucky moccasins, that I had purchased in Albuquerque, were coming apart. I said, "Yes, I know. But I cannot do anything about it". The kind American replied, "I have got needles and cotton in my room. I guess I could repair them in time". We went along. One thing led to another and finally she said, "Isn't it going to affect you in the race tomorrow, wasting time and energy like this?" I said I did not think it would.'

Lewis may well have forgiven Jumbo for endangering their partnership by piloting a stricken aeroplane just days before they left England, but Jumbo wisely kept this energetic escapade in the hotel to himself. His moccasins though were as good as new, and did seem to bring luck.

It was the morning of the 10th, and Jumbo and Lewis woke up early and went for a light training row. The time for their coxless pairs heat was 3 p.m., and there were five other nations up against them. They were

Hugh and Lewis return from a training row on the Olympic course at Long Beach © Jack Beresford's Family.

drawn in heat two, alongside Stiles and Thompson of New Zealand, and Roelofsen and Roëll of the Netherlands. Jumbo and Lewis were wary – before the heat Jumbo had stressed his fear of the Dutch, 'In the pairs our most serious opposition, I should say, are the Dutch and the French. The Dutch are champions of Europe.' They had also seen the Kiwi pair in training, and were impressed.

Jumbo and Lewis were wary but also supremely confident. They were the undefeated pair for the past two years at Henley, and were in the very prime of fitness. They complemented one another. 'Lewis supplied the guts and the power while I supplied the finesse and watermanship', was Jumbo's evaluation of the magic that they could produce on the water. However, the world's Press were favouring the European champions, the Dutch.

The Daily Telegraph played down any hopes for the coxless pair, 'Great Britain's rowing eight and the sculler, Southwood, are heralded here as the most likely winners of this week's rowing events'.

The three pairs lined up at the start. A large crowd had flocked to the course and were lining the sandy banks and packed into the stadium at

Luck of the Moccasins

the finish line. Jumbo took a deep breath and closed his eyes. Then the shout of 'Partez' from the starter.

The Dutch started well, and after the first few strokes had a slight lead over New Zealand and the British pair. Then Jumbo and Lewis settled into their accustomed rhythm of 'power and finesse'. At the 400 metre marker they had made up the short deficit and were slightly ahead of the two other boats. Lewis and Jumbo upped their stroke rate once more, and at 600 metres they had established a length's lead over the New Zealanders.

To the surprise of many, the Dutch European Champions were struggling with the pace set by the Brits. New Zealand reacted to the lengthening gap, they increased their stroke rate to an impressive thirty-six against Jumbo and Lewis at thirty. At the halfway mark, 1,000 metres, New Zealand had fought back and were level. The Dutch were two lengths back. It was now between the Kiwis and the Brits for the victory and an automatic advance into the final. The two boats were side by side with 300 metres to go, but with the noise of the cheers of the crowd in the stadium drifting up the water, Jumbo and Lewis reacted.

The crowd were on their feet. George Drinkwater was yelling from the bank. Jumbo and Lewis were in perfect rowing harmony.

They crossed the finish line half a length in front of the trailing and struggling New Zealanders, with the Dutch a distant third.

The British pair were into the final, with a time of seven minutes and forty seconds. This was thirteen seconds faster than the Polish pair who had won the first heat, narrowly pipping the fancied French, with the Americans third.

Jumbo was slightly taken aback at the ease of their win. There was just one problem – he had only an hour to recover before he was transported back up the course to climb into the coxless four.

'We won our heat in the pair comfortably, but in the fours we had no yardstick by which to judge our speed.'

A tanned Hugh, his hair bleached blonde by the Californian sun and wearing his Great Britain Olympic jersey, is photographed by Jack Beresford at Long Beach © Jack Beresford's Family.

The four were drawn in a tough heat against two of the more fancied crews that were seen as a threat against the British: the Americans and the Germans. Prior to the regatta, the British four were regarded as narrow favourites. Beresford and Badcock had won silver four years previously in the British eight, and the Thames four had dominated Henley. However, with Tyler's absence from the boat this was no longer the Thames four – and the Press had declared his absence as a 'major blow to any hope'. But the remaining Thames three had supreme confidence in Jumbo – they had competed against him so many times and, more importantly, there was a friendship and trust in his ability to row twice in an hour. They had witnessed his remarkable hat-trick of victories at Henley the previous year.

For Jumbo there was a sudden instant of relief. A gentle and cooling wind had sprung up and the British boat had been drawn on the sheltered station, which protected them from a freshening northwester.

All three boats started strongly. By the 150 metre mark the British four had edged ahead. When a quarter of the distance had been rowed, Germany were only half a length behind, with the United States a length away in third. The Germans pulled strongly, and at the halfway mark they were back level with Great Britain, but the onlookers could see that the British four were rowing much more smoothly and had a greater reserve.

From this point the race was as good as over. To the delight of the partisan crowd, the Americans passed the tiring Germans to finish second behind the British.

The British four had cruised into the final, three lengths up on the Americans in a time of seven minutes and thirteen seconds. In the other heat, with only two nations competing, the strong Italian four defeated the Canadians in a very impressive time of seven minutes and six seconds. The Italians were impressively fast.

An exhausted – but triumphant – Jumbo returned with the team to the joy of a hot bath and a welcoming bed. In three days' time Jumbo would attempt a feat that only one other rower in Olympic history had ever achieved, two gold medals in one day.

In 1920, Jack Kelly was the supreme single sculler in the United States. Jack wished to test himself against the best of the European scullers and applied to race in the Diamond Challenge Sculls at Henley Royal Regatta. The event's organisers rejected his application, citing the fact that he had once worked as a manual labourer with his brother's construction firm – 'Mr Kelly was not qualified under Rule I(e) of the General Rules (manual labour)'.

At that time, Henley had strict rules on those who were allowed to compete. Having performed manual labour was one such baffling rule that could not be breached.

On learning of his rejection, Kelly was surprised and rightly angered: 'I had made all the arrangements to sail for England... I'll go to the Olympics now for sure. I want to get a crack at the man who wins the Diamond Sculls.'

Kelly soon had his chance. At the 1920 Summer Olympics in Antwerp, Kelly was representing the United States. Awaiting him in the single sculls final was Britain's Jack Beresford – the recent winner of the Diamond Challenge Sculls at Henley. The final, one of the closest in Olympic history, featured a dramatic duel down the last stretch of water with Kelly just pipping Beresford at the line. Kelly had his revenge on the British. Having proven their joint supremacy in the single sculls, the two Jacks would go on to become good friends.

Half an hour after the Olympic final of the singles sculls, Jack Kelly teamed with his cousin Paul Costello to win the double sculls race. Now, twelve years later, Jack Beresford could help Jumbo achieve what his good friend Jack Kelly, father of Grace Kelly, had – double gold.

The day of the finals was bathed in the Californian sunshine to which the rowers had grown accustomed. It was Saturday, August 13th, and all seven rowing finals were scheduled to commence at 3 p.m.

Two days previously, the repechage of the coxless pairs and coxless fours had taken place. In the pairs, the Dutch had found their form and won. Coming second, and joining the Dutch, were the New Zealanders – eliminating the French and Americans. Jumbo and Lewis would be up against the same two teams that they had defeated in their heat, along with the powerful Polish pair who had won their heat and also automatically qualified.

In the fours, the Germans and Americans were victorious in their repechage – and so, as with the pairs, Jumbo would be up against two teams that he had already beaten in the heats. The Italians, who won the other heat, would be the fourth finalists. A psychological battle had perhaps already been won.

For Tig Tyler there was to be heartbreak. Tig had been unable to train and although now feeling better he was finally told by George Drinkwater that he would not be returning to the boat – the rulebook did not allow it. Tig was also aware that Jumbo had fitted seamlessly into the four.

Tig's Olympic Games were over; they had never started. It was calamitous for him.

Jumbo spent the morning walking the two kilometre length of the course by himself. He wanted solitude. He sat by the lagoon and looked across to the oil derricks that dominated the far bank. He closed his eyes and in his mind he went through the race, visualising the strokes, feeling the boat gliding beneath him, hearing the boat sing.

The first of the finals that Jumbo would compete in would be the pairs, followed shortly by a mad dash back up the course for the fours.

All of the British rowing crews had made it to the final day, across four of the disciplines. As well as Jumbo in the pairs and fours, Dick Southwood was in the single sculls final and the eight had made it through to the final as well.

Unlike the other British rowers, the highly fancied Cambridge eight had struggled to make it through to their final. In their heat they faced Italy, Japan and Brazil. Only Italy posed a threat, but even then the Press were fully confident that the eight who had rowed so beautifully in the Boat Race and then at Henley would cruise through. It wasn't to be. After a problematic start, the crew settled into a rhythm to be leading at halfway. However, the Italians stormed back and won easily by two lengths from the British.

In the repechage, the British eight made no further mistakes and they beat New Zealand with a length to spare. Great Britain and the United States were the dominant nations in this blue riband event of the regatta, with the two nations winning all seven prior Olympic men's eight-oared competitions between them. The United States held a 5–2 edge and were the reigning champions, having beaten the British team in the final in 1928 to take their third straight gold.

The eights final would be contested between Great Britain, United States, Italy and an outsider, Canada.

First up in the finals for the British team would be Dick Southwood in the single sculls, followed by Jumbo and Lewis in the coxless pairs, Jumbo and the Thames Three in the coxless fours and culminating in the eights.

It was estimated by the newspapers that 75,000 spectators had descended onto Long Beach and the Marine Stadium. Tickets had sold out, and the crowds who had not gained entry to the stands lining the final hundred metres of the course had made their way to the banks, jostling for the best views. On either side of the two-kilometre course, workers had climbed the oil derricks – perching precariously on the steel framework to get the ideal view of the racing.

At 3 p.m. it was time for the single sculls final and Dick Southwood. Dick was up against the defending Olympic champion, Bobby Pearce, the American Bill Miller and the outsider, Uruguayan Guillermo Douglas who had negotiated the repechage. Uruguay had never had a rower at the Olympic Games, and Douglas was beaming proudly as he manoeuvred his boat into the start position. The Australian Pearce was the dominant force in single sculls and it was thought that the gold medal would be fought out between himself and Dick. However, Bill Miller certainly had a vociferous support and had pushed Pearce to the limit in their heat.

Accompanied by a terrific roar, the race started and Pearce quickly established a narrow lead over Miller, with Dick third. At the halfway mark the order remained the same and it was looking to be the close race that everyone expected. Pearce and Miller continued to set the pace, but Dick was fading. Douglas was doing the unthinkable and was catching, and then passing, Dick with ease. With the crowd focussing on Pearce and Miller, only the British team could see that Dick was cramping up and his rhythm had disappeared.

Bobby Pearce held on from a battling Miller, and won by three quarters of a length, defending his Olympic title. Douglas finished third, a good four or five lengths down from second placed Miller. Dick could only paddle his way to the finish line. He was a good half a minute behind Douglas.

Britain had got off to the worst possible start of the finals, and Dick was distraught. For Douglas, he would return home to Uruguay with his bronze medal and a hero's welcome. Bobby Pearce would drive the three thousand miles back to Ontario with his boat on the roof of his car and a gold medal around his neck.

Four years later in Berlin, Dick Southwood would gain redemption.

Along with Jack Beresford he won a dramatic double sculls final for his Olympic gold medal. They did so in front of the watching glare of Adolf Hitler.

Next up in the finals was the coxless pair of Jumbo and Lewis.

They had both experienced finals at Henley, they had both competed in the Boat Race. But this was different. It felt different. This was for their country. It was also a moment of supreme trust in one another. As a pair they worked as a whole. When the coaches watched them row, it was a beautiful sight. As Jumbo had summed up their partnership: they were 'power and finesse'.

They had already vanquished the Netherlands and the New Zealanders in their heat, but the other finalists Poland were to be feared. They could not be complacent.

Jumbo and Lewis positioned their boat at the start. They had been drawn in the nearside lane, closest to the bank. Adjacent to them were the New Zealand pair. Lewis called out, 'We've got this Jum'. Then complete silence.

The starter called out to the boats in the traditional French. "Messieurs, etes vous pret?... Partez!".

The four boats were quick off the start but it was the Poles who soon established a lead. Jumbo and Lewis were not panicking, they held a steady rhythm. At the five hundred metre mark, Poland were ahead of the British pair by a length, with New Zealand a further length back in third.

When Jumbo and Lewis had walked the course the previous day they had stopped at this five hundred metre mark and looked down the water to the grandstands. This was where they were going to put on a spurt.

The British pair upped their stroke rate to thirty-two – their oars moving beautifully through the water. At the halfway marker, they glided past the Polish pair. They were now at the front and extending their lead over a tiring Poland. The New Zealand pair of Thompson and Stiles responded but it was too late to make any difference.

Hugh and Lewis approach the winning post, ahead of New Zealand, in the final of the Olympic coxless pairs.

Jumbo and Lewis swept past the winning post. They had won by a length, in a time of eight minutes exactly. They had won gold. New Zealand won silver, and a determined Polish pair held off the Dutch to win bronze. Jumbo was an Olympic champion.

Jumbo and Lewis clambered out of the boat and shook hands in a typically understated British show of emotion. In truth, there was no time for Jumbo to reflect on what they had achieved and to celebrate their victory – he had to join Jack Beresford, Felix Badcock and Rowland George and prepare for the coxless four final.

There was just time for cursory congratulations between the victorious pair and George Drinkwater, but Jumbo's concentration was now required for the upcoming race. There was not even any time to change his sweat-drenched shirt.

Just half an hour after Jumbo had won Olympic gold, he was two kilometres back up to the start of the course, in a boat preparing for the coxless four final.

Facing the British four were the two crews that they had defeated in the heats. The Germans of Karl Aletter, Ernst Gaber, Walter Flinsch and

The Great Britain coxless four row to victory in the final. From left-to-right: John Badcock, Jack Beresford, Hugh, and Rowland George © Thames Rowing Club.

Hans Maier were considered by the rowing aficionado as the main threat to the British but had been well beaten in the heats by both Britain and the Americans. The American four of John McCosker, George Mattson, Thomas Pierie and Edgar Johnson were the crew from Pennsylvania Athletic Club, the Philadelphia rowing club directed by Jack Kelly – the Olympian that Jumbo was hoping to emulate with a successive victory in this race. The fourth nation competing for gold were the Italians of Antonio Garzoni Provenzani, Giliante D'Este, Francesco Cossu and Antonio Ghiardello. The Italians had won their heat by a couple of lengths, bettering the time that the British set in their heat by over six seconds. The parting words of Jumbo to Lewis when he headed back up the course were, 'We have tough opposition'.

In the British boat Felix Badcock (at stroke), Jack Beresford, Jumbo and Rowland George readied themselves. They needed a good start to undermine further the confidence of the two crews that they had already bettered in the heats. As with the coxless pair, the British boat had been drawn in the nearside lane closest to the bank.

Once again Jumbo closed his eyes, steadied his breathing and concentrated on the French words of the starter. "Partez!".

In Jumbo's words, 'We were off. Running up to full speed after five strokes, I knew we were going to win. There was a tremendous feeling of speed, of power, and a determination to win. At no time did I feel we were not in control. It was beautiful.'

New Zealand did try to come back at the British four but it was a procession for the entire two kilometres of the course. The British four eased past the winning post to the cheers from the grandstands.

They had won by two and a half lengths, in a time of six minutes and fifty-eight seconds. Germany and Italy fought it out for silver, with the Germans just managing to hold off the Italians.

To the disappointment of the partisan crowd, and the watching Jack Kelly, the United States finished last but the spectators gave Jumbo the longest ovation of the regatta. What inspired the onlookers was not only his endurance, but the element of sacrificial bravery wound into his endeavours in the boat. His second victory unfolded in front of them like the plot of some dramatic Hollywood movie.

High up in the stands and sitting next to the jubilant British team, Tig Tyler wept. He shared their pride but the tears were of bitter disappointment of what could have been.

Chapter 12

Achieving the Impossible

Hugh 'Jumbo' Edwards had just achieved what most thought impossible. In under an hour, in two strength-sapping finals, he had won two gold medals. As he sat in the boat, gulping down Californian air and trying to recover his strength, he glanced back up the course. The sun was low in the sky, and the late afternoon rays bathed the grandstands. The water gleamed gold.

The four clambered out of the boat, and quickly congratulated one another. A photographer immediately approached them with a request for the Olympic champions to stand on the dock, oars aloft. They stood there – rigidly – with barely a flicker of a triumphant smile. George, Beresford and Badcock were wearing their Great Britain vests, shorts and Thames Rowing Club socks. Jumbo had discarded his now sweat-sodden Great Britain vest and had quickly changed into the shirt he wore for Oxford in the Boat Race. His initials 'H. R. A. E.' were emblazoned on the front instead of the Union Jack, and he was not wearing socks.

There was a look of defiance on Jumbo's tanned face. The 25-year-old who had lost the Boat Race for Oxford six years previously, who had been told never to row again, was a double Olympic champion.

One of the many innovations that had been introduced in Los Angeles for the Xth Olympic Games was a podium for the medallists. An exhausted Jumbo climbed atop of the winning step twice, the British national anthem blaring triumphantly across the stadium as the immense crowd rose to their feet.

The Great Britain winning coxless four. From left-to-right: Rowland George, Jack Beresford, Hugh and John Badcock.

Back home in England, the news of the remarkable double win was reported in the next day's newspapers. However, a reader would be hard pressed to find the story – and even then there was no mention in any of the newspapers of two golds in one day. The sports pages of the newspapers were dominated with horse racing, junior tennis and rugby.

When the Olympic rowing was reported on, most of the papers led with a humiliating last place for the Great Britain eight in the signature event of the rowing programme. To the raucous delight of the 75,000 crowd, the United States had won the most thrilling of eights finals – just edging out the Italians. A typical headline on the sports page was 'Cambridge Eight Fail – But Coxless Fours Won by Great Britain' (*Yorkshire Post*). The report contained a single paragraph, 'One of the most easily-won Olympic titles fell to the British four. The chief interest was not so much who would win, but who would fill the position runners-up.'

There were no front page headlines of a unique achievement by a British athlete. Cinema goers were, however, presented with a brief one-minute Pathé News clip of the coxless four victory. The newsreel with American commentary was entitled 'Something we **did** win!' and shows the four

Achieving the Impossible

gliding smoothly, and unopposed, over the finishing line – countless oil derricks and the massed crowds forming the background.

The following day, on Sunday August 14th, the Olympics were officially ended with the Closing Ceremony. Over the fortnight, 1,871 athletes had competed across fourteen sports, from thirty-seven nations. The United States topped the medal table with a dominant forty-one gold medals, and Great Britain finished in a very commendable eighth place with four gold, seven silver and five bronze medals. Jumbo was fundamental to half of the gold medals won by Great Britain.

With pageantry to match the Opening Ceremony, the athletes watched on as the Olympic flame was extinguished and the Olympic flag lowered, ready to be delivered to Berlin for the 1936 Games.

With the Olympics finished, the British team could relax. They readily accepted an invitation out to Hollywood and a lavish party hosted at the mansion of Douglas Fairbanks and his wife Mary Pickford. Then it was time to pack bags and begin the long journey back home.

'The teams dispersed, some members staying on in the States, others returning via San Francisco or other routes', recalled Jumbo. 'I returned with three or four others via Salt Lake City, where we had an extraordinary swim in the Great Salt Lake. Travelling back across the continent was a wearisome business. I returned across the Atlantic on the *Empress of Britain*. Joyce Cooper, who won bronze in the women's 100 metre relay, was also on board. She tried to teach me the crawl, and very nearly succeeded in teaching me the backstroke.'

Two years later, Joyce would go on to marry Jumbo's fellow gold medallist in the coxless four, John 'Felix' Badcock. They would remain close friends throughout their lives.

On arrival back in Southampton, there was no great fanfare to welcome home the returning Olympic hero. However, at Waterloo station there was a crowd to greet the team. On disembarking the boat train, the crowd surged forward to hang laurel wreaths around the necks of Lord Burghley

The Olympic Diploma awarded to Hugh in recognition of his two gold medals in the coxless pair and the coxless four.

and Tommy Hampson – the 800-metre champion. So intent was the crowd on showering their congratulations on the athletic pair that Jumbo was able to hurriedly get away from the platform. In all truth, the apathy towards rowing at the Olympics meant that the public would be hard-pressed to recognise the double Olympic champion in their midst.

Jumbo exited the station and hailed a taxi back to Kensington and a reunion with his mother, his brothers and sister.

At the age of twenty-five, Jumbo had achieved all that he desired from rowing.

In *The Times*, Gully Nickalls – who had been one of Jumbo's harshest critics – at last paid tribute to his talent: 'H. R. A. Edwards is the finest oarsman of his generation'.

Jumbo had laid to rest the failure of 1926.

'On my return to England I now decided to give up rowing. I had perfected my rowing to the highest degree of which I was capable, and the rowing world had no more prizes to offer. I ceased to take any further interest in the sport. Flying had now become my major interest.'

Chapter 13

Call me Mike

By the end of 1932, Jumbo was a serving flying officer in the Royal Air Force. His graduation from Oxford had allowed him to gain his commission to RAF 17th Squadron. He was posted to Upavon, sixteen miles north of Salisbury in Wiltshire.

Upavon was a grass airfield, military flight training school and administrative headquarters of the Royal Air Force. The days were spent training as a pilot, with most flights restricted to a radius of ten miles from the airfield. Jumbo practised various types of flight attacks using a camera gun, with which the accuracy of the pilot could be assessed. The squadron went through numerous formation flying exercises and, for Jumbo, the more exhilarating manoeuvre of dive bombing.

To alleviate the pressure of training, Jumbo and his fellow officers would venture into Salisbury. He had stumbled upon a tearoom called *Michael's Lyttle Shoppe*. Jumbo settled in for some tea and cake, and asked the beguiling waitress who Michael was. 'I am' came the swift reply. She was small, dark haired and spirited. Jumbo was instantly smitten.

'Michael ("call me Mike") was a remarkable woman. She had opened up the tea shop with her girl friend, Terry Hann, in order to get away

A sketch of Michael's Lyttle Shoppe, Salisbury, where Hugh first met Mike, 1929.

from her possessive mother. The girls ran it more in the style of a courtesan's salon than as a money-making business.'

After that first meeting, Jumbo became a frequent customer – and Mike did not allow the Olympic champion to pay for anything. Mike was from a military family. Her father, John 'Jack' Williams, had spent his life in the army, rising to the rank of Major, and it was when he was stationed in Malta that 'Michael' was born. The family story has it that Jack was so determined to have a boy that his disappointment on the arrival of a daughter was tempered by his wife Agnes allowing him to refer to their daughter as 'Michael'. Mike was born in 1899 – baptised as Lydia Rose Williams – and was thirty-three years of age when Jumbo first walked into *Michael's Lyttle Shoppe*. However, she did not reveal her true age – she told Jumbo that she was twenty-five – an astonishing eight years younger than she was. Her actual age, and baptised name, was a secret that Mike never revealed to her family-to-be.

There was a tradition in Mike's family for alterations in names and birth dates. In 1888, Mike's father enlisted in the army under his birth name John Frederick Tacagni. John was second-generation Italian, the Tacagnis had emigrated from a village near Lake Como and established a furniture business in Shoreditch, London. When John enlisted with the army he stated his age as nineteen. He was in fact only fourteen. His army career only lasted two months – he was sent up to Newcastle-upon-Tyne to serve with the Durham Light Infantry but homesickness resulted in John heading back to London and paying his way out of service. However, nine months later he had once again joined up with the army – he enrolled under the changed surname of Williams. This time he persevered with army life, and he remained in the military for forty years until his retirement in 1928.

Jumbo would try his best to impress Mike with flights above the Wiltshire countryside. A man of passions, he now had one more to rival the flying.

In April 1933, Jumbo transferred to 600 Bomber Squadron at RAF Hendon – an airbase just north of London. This resulted in seeing less of Mike, but whenever he had free time he would fly out to Salisbury to visit the tea room.

At Hendon, Jumbo would spend most of his time putting the Hawker Hart – a fast, two-seater biplane, day bomber – through its paces.

Michael Williams as a young woman in Salisbury (age unknown).

Whilst Jumbo was roaring through the skies, pairs partner Lewis Clive had realised that a career in banking was not suited to his sense of adventure. A month before Jumbo transferred to Hendon, Lewis was back on an ocean liner heading across the Atlantic. This time it was not the sultry heat of California that he was aiming for, it was the snow and intense cold of the Canadian Northwest Territories.

Lewis had signed up with the explorer and meteorologist James H. Martin to study Arctic weather conditions and to map one hundred and fifty square miles of unexplored territory north of the Great Slave Lake. After seven weeks using a husky sled to transport themselves over the snow, they arrived back at their Alberta base with only two dogs out of their original team of five.

When Lewis arrived back in England from his Arctic exploration he immediately pleaded with Jumbo to get back in the boat. Lewis argued that it was their duty to defend their Silver Goblets title at Henley.

Despite neither of them having rowed since the Olympics, Lewis had a strong belief that the magic of the partnership could be rekindled – that they could bring back the power and finesse that had made them the most feared pair in the world. Jumbo relented. He took one week's leave from the RAF and they had two days of practice before the start of Henley Royal Regatta.

With July weather reminiscent of Los Angeles, the feared Olympic champions took to the water against A. P. Brown and J. H. M. Ward of Thames Rowing Club. Despite their lack of practice, Jumbo and Lewis won by half a length. In the next heat, they took on the Bigland brothers of the Royal Chester Rowing Club. Jumbo and Lewis, the Olympic champions and holders of the Silver Goblets, were soundly beaten.

Jumbo vowed never to get back into a boat and race. Instead, he went down on one knee and proposed to Mike. She said yes.

Flying and Mike were his priorities. He was finished with the river.

Jumbo was the middle brother of three. Sphinx was his elder by just over a year, and John – always known by his middle name, Oswald – was five years younger. In 1933, Oswald, aged twenty-one, was studying at Oxford but had opted not to follow in the Christ Church tradition of his two brothers and instead enrolled at Keble College. Keble had been founded in the 1860s to promote cheaper education for High Church clergymen and their sons and Oswald benefitted from this connection. He had always loved to watch his brothers compete on the river and in the Boat Race, and this family rowing gene had also been inherited by him. Oswald was selected at stroke to compete in the trials for the Oxford eight. However, he ultimately missed out on the final selection and to be the third Edwards to earn his Blue. His talent as an oarsman was not in doubt, and in 1933 he competed at Henley in the Diamond Challenge Sculls.

On graduation that year, Oswald did not follow his brothers into the RAF but instead he took up a commission into the army as Second Lieutenant for the East Surrey Regiment. Their mother back in Kensington now had all three sons serving, and pursuing military careers.

With all of the intensive RAF training, Jumbo had very little time to do any private flying. Consequently he did not feel that he was prepared enough to enter that year's King's Cup. His brother Sphinx, who was also establishing himself as a highly rated Flight Lieutenant for the RAF, did enter. For this year's race, Viscountess Hardinge had entered her plane – a Comper Swift – and had employed Sphinx as the pilot. It would be one of the most exciting finishes in the history of the King's Cup.

> 'Captain Geoffrey de Havilland – a pioneer of flying – won the King's Cup air race at Hatfield, Herts, on Saturday. Flying only a couple of hundred feet or so above the ground, he made a last final bid and passed the winning line not much more than twenty or thirty feet in front of Flight Lieutenant E. C. T. 'Sphinx' Edwards. It was such a fine race that there was not more than four minutes between the winner's time and that of the last man. Only one of the 35 entrants was injured. His plane crashed.' (*Leeds Mercury*)

On June 16th, 1934, Jumbo and Mike were married in Salisbury. *The Times* reported that the marriage would 'take place quietly in the countryside'. On the marriage certificate, Mike continued her deception about her real age and stated that her birth year was 1907 and not 1899.

Jumbo and Mike settled into married life, with Jumbo continuing to progress through the ranks in the RAF. He was appointed Flying Officer in July that year and would often take Mike as his passenger on pleasure flights around the country and across the Channel.

Much to the displeasure of Mike, Jumbo did opt to leave the new marital home a month after the wedding to compete in the King's Cup. The last time he entered, in 1932, he crash landed – and Mike was understandably fearing a similar outcome.

Flying his Martlet Gypsy, Jumbo finished sixth – a place behind the defending champion Geoffrey de Havilland. More importantly he returned home intact.

The following year, in 1935, both brothers entered the King's Cup. This would be the first time that Jumbo and Sphinx had raced against one another since 1932.

The development of aircraft in the mid-1930s was continuing at a brisk pace. New, more powerful, engines were being developed and the double-wing biplane that had dominated the design of aeroplanes was being replaced with the more stream-lined monoplanes. By 1935 the race was regularly being won by the new breed of racing aeroplanes like the Percival Gull, eventually averaging well over 200 mph.

A close friend of the brothers was F. G. (Fredrerick) Miles, a racing pilot but also an emerging aircraft designer and manufacturer. Sphinx had purchased his first aeroplane from Miles – the Avro Baby (G-EAUM registration) – which he then sold to Jumbo. In the 1935 King's Cup, almost half of all the entrants were flying aeroplanes designed and manufactured by F. G. Miles.

Jumbo had swapped his Martlet Gypsy biplane (also designed by Miles) for the faster monoplane Miles M.2R Hawk Major that was owned by a friend, R. Cornwall. The Edwards brothers were up against aviators with whom they were all very familiar, and against whom they raced on a regular basis. Aviators such as Geoffrey de Havilland, Captain Percival (Prince Edward's official pilot and the winner in 1934) and Tommy Rose were also joined by F. G. Miles and at twenty-one years of age the youngest competitor, Alex Henshaw.

The qualification for the final went smoothly for Jumbo. The course took the flyers from Hatfield Aerodrome, in London, north to Edinburgh, over Glasgow, out to Belfast, south to Cardiff and then back to Hatfield. Jumbo covered the 953 miles in just over six hours – behind the aeroplanes of F. G. Miles and Captain Percival who qualified in the two quickest times. Sphinx's Percival D.2 Gull developed engine problems and he was forced to retire at Belfast.

Alex Henshaw met with a far more dramatic conclusion to his race. Over the Irish sea, having just departed from Belfast, Henshaw's Miles

Hawker experienced mechanical issues with the crankshaft. In Henshaw's own words, 'At about two thousand feet my machine quickly lost speed and altitude. Finding that a crash was inevitable, I steered for a steamer ship that I could see. My aeroplane fell into the sea about a quarter of a mile away from her, and I was shot out of the cockpit into the water. I swam back to the 'plane and stood upon the wing until the lifeboat from the steamer rescued me'.

Henshaw's dramatic rescue was witnessed by two hundred holidaymakers on board the steamer. His only injury was a bruised leg. The country owed a debt of gratitude to the steamer. At the outset of the Second World War, Alex Henshaw would go on to become the supreme test pilot for Vickers Armstrong. Henshaw would put countless Spitfires and Lancasters through their paces at the Castle Bromwich aeroplane factory where he personally flight tested over three thousand of the Spitfires manufactured at the plant.

On Saturday, September 7th, the King's Cup finalists took off from Hatfield Aerodrome. For the final day, the twenty aeroplanes that had qualified had to cover the fifty-mile triangular course six times. A reporter for the press thrillingly recounted the race.

'With all the competitors in the air, the race became full of thrills and high speed excitement. Thousands of spectators gasped as competitors came to the turn immediately above their heads. The pilots put their machines to the most perilous angles in order to take the corner in the shortest time, then shooting away, increasing their speed almost every lap.'

As the spectators looked on, Flight Lieutenant Tommy Rose, who was placed eleventh at the end of the first lap, quickly overtook his rivals and was up into third place by the fourth lap. He was closely followed by the faster pilots, amongst them Jumbo who was now averaging almost 180 mph and in fifth position.

The excitement grew as the pilots completed each circuit of the course. At the end of the fourth lap, the first six were all in close pursuit. Jumbo

The Miles M.2R Hawk Major, flown by Hugh, sitting in the hangar before the start of the King's Cup Air Race, 1935.

had dropped back and was placed sixth. The Australian, Gus Tweddle, who had led during the first four laps, dropped back to tenth at the start of the fifth, and penultimate, lap.

Going into the final lap Tommy Rose was leading, followed by Lieutenant Cathcart-Jones. Jumbo had recovered and was timing his race to perfection: he was up to third and closing in on the leader. As the crowds scanned the horizon for the returning planes, it was Tommy Rose in his Miles Falcon who roared across the finish line. The plane now tearing towards the finish line to take second was a Miles M.2R Hawk Major. Both Jumbo and Cathcart-Jones were flying a Hawk Major. Flashing low over the grass field of the aerodrome was the aeroplane with the number G-ADLN. Jumbo had finished second.

Although he was perhaps more used to winning important finals, for Jumbo achieving a second place in the premier air race was an achievement of great pride. However, Sphinx was quick to remind his younger brother that he had not quite matched his winning achievement of four years before.

Jumbo returned home to Mike and their six-month-old baby son. John Hugh Michael Edwards was born in March 1935, at the family home in Elsham Road, Kensington.

A month prior to the King's Cup Air Race – in August 1935 – Sphinx was sent on a special assignment to Germany. With the rise to power of the National Socialist German Workers' Party under Adolf Hitler, there was obvious concern in Europe over the expansion and rearmament of the German army, navy and airforce.

In June 1935, Hitler sent a German delegation led by Joachim von Ribbentrop to London to negotiate an Anglo-German Naval Agreement. This was an ambitious attempt on the part of both the British and the Germans to reach better relations. For Germany, the Anglo-German Naval Agreement was intended to mark the beginning of an Anglo-German alliance against France and the Soviet Union. For Britain, the Agreement was to be the beginning of a series of arms limitations to put a hold on German expansionism.

After the discussions were concluded, von Ribbentrop invited the British Government to send over representatives from the navy – and the RAF – for a tour of Germany to inspect the ports and airfields. Included within this small delegation was Sphinx who, along with his main posting as a Flight Lieutenant with the RAF, had been appointed to the Directorate of Organization in the Air Ministry. It was felt that Sphinx's friendship with German aviators – he had raced many Luftwaffe pilots in European competitions over the past few years – as well as his fame as a racing pilot would be advantageous.

In a letter to his mother, Sphinx provided a few details of what he was experiencing in a Germany that was now being transformed by the rise of the Nazi Party. On letter headed paper from the Hotel Der Achtermann, located in the town of Goslar, Lower Saxony, Sphinx neatly wrote:

> 'The next afternoon in Berlin we were taken in a huge Nazi party car, complete with a black-clad Storm Trooper driver in full uni-

form, to see Potsdam, the lakes and anywhere else in the neighbourhood we wished. This was provided by von Ribbentrop – one of Hitler's right-hand men.

We were afterwards given an excellent dinner and unlimited Moselle to drink on the shores of the Wannsee.

I think we created a considerable stir in the hotel when they saw us being driven off in a 'party car', and I feel that the manager, had we afterwards refused to pay the bill, would have uttered only the feeblest of protests.

We also had lunch that day with young O.W. who used to cox Hugh and I: he is now finishing a tour of three years at the Embassy in Berlin. He had some interesting things to say about the Nazis and others. We dined in the Kurfürstendamm where most of the recent Jew-baiting took place.'

Sphinx returned to England, reported to his superiors about what they were 'allowed' to see, and hoped that the rise of fascism and anti-Semitism that he had witnessed could somehow be curtailed.

The Anglo-German Naval Agreement ultimately foundered and in 1937 Sphinx was promoted to Squadron Leader. He was assigned to No. 23 (Training) Group to help train the pilots and navigators that – it was feared – would soon be needed. With the emergence of Hitler, Mussolini and General Franco – the rise of the far right in Europe made the modernisation of Britain's armed forces imperative.

Lewis Clive had returned from his exploration of the Northwestern Territories a changed man. The Etonian who was a member of the Bullingdon Club and son of a Conservative MP had time to contemplate his plans for the future whilst mapping out territory on the husky sled. Lewis rebelled against the politics of his father and became an active member of the centre-left Labour Party. As the rowing historian Tim Koch summarised, 'Lewis became a Labour Party member of the Council in the seemingly comfortable London Borough of Kensington and also a member of the Fabian Society. The Fabians advocated gradual rather than revolutionary change and its membership was almost entirely composed of upper middle-class intellectuals.'

At one of London's soup kitchens, Lewis was to meet and fall in love with one of the volunteers – Mary Farmar. As with Lewis, Mary was from an upper-class family – her maternal grandmother was Lady Dalby – and at the age of eighteen she had been presented at court. Soon after, Mary was volunteering to help the poor and underprivileged. She and Lewis were also develop-

Lewis Clive, shortly before he left for Spain and the Civil War © Clive Family.

ing a close friendship. Lewis was smitten with this beautiful young kindred spirit and proposed to Mary. But the marriage proposal was refused and she soon grew bored both with Lewis and with political meetings, and in January 1937 – needing to get away from her overbearing parents – she married a wealthy young peer, Charles Swinfen Eady.

Lewis was devastated but he soon met and fell in love with Elisabeth Wilkinson, a left-wing journalist who had been in Guernica during April 1937 when the Spanish town was devastated by Nazi Germany's Luftwaffe and the Italian Aviazione Legionaria. She managed to escape the bombs and returned to England to tell the newspapers of the devastation.

In 1938, with his continuing quest for adventure, Lewis was determined not to be dismissed and mocked as one of those 'champagne socialists'. With encouragement from his barrister friend, John Platts-Mills, and Elisabeth Wilkinson, Lewis enlisted with the British Battalion of the

15th International Brigade. At the age of twenty-seven, Lewis was on his way to Spain to fight the Nationalists of General Franco.

Lewis was soon proving his bravery. As *The Times* detailed, 'Earlier in the campaign he had a remarkable escape when, after an overwhelming advance of Italian tanks, he found himself cut off behind the enemy lines, but succeeded in crawling back to his own lines after ten days of great privation'. As Tim Koch revealed, in all probability this refers to an incident in March 1938 when six hundred and fifty men from the 15th Brigade marched into a column of Italian soldiers. Only eighty Brigaders made it back to their own lines. Lewis was quickly promoted to the rank of Commander of 2nd Company.

In July, the Battle of the Ebro commenced. Lewis Clive was once again in a boat, this time rowing his comrades across the fast-flowing River Ebro at Ascó on July 25th. The weary battalion quickly advanced to Corbera. The following day the town of Gandesa was attacked but the Nationalists held out and no further progress was made.

On the 29th, under a burning sun, the battalion attacked once more. Confronting them was the steep incline of Hill 418. There was only limited cover for the troops, a few pine trees amongst the scree and rosemary. Lewis led his company, slowly, up the hill – they were under constant fire from the Nationalists. During a lull in the shooting, Lewis broke cover to try and get a better understanding of where the enemy had positioned themselves.

George Wheeler, one of Lewis's men, was crouching down next to Lewis. 'At that moment I felt splashes on my left forearm, and glancing down, was astonished to see they were splashes of blood. Turning, I saw Lewis reel and fall.'

Lewis had been shot in the head by a Nationalist sniper. His death was instantaneous.

Ballads were, and are still, sung about the exploits of the International Brigades and in particular the Company Commander, Lewis Clive:

> *When Lewis Clive became a man*
> *his back was straight, his arms were strong*
> *And he became an Oxford blue and then in 1932*
> *Beneath the Californian sun the umpire fired the starting gun*
> *And the rings were blazing bright and bold*
> *when Lewis won Olympic Gold*
> *(Young 'Uns, from the Album 'The Ballad of Johnny Longstaff)*

In 1984, Mary Farmar – the woman that Lewis had fallen in love with – published a novel under her pseudonym: Mary Wesley. The novel was the bestselling *The Camomile Lawn*. One of the main protagonists, Oliver, was a man who falls in love but when rejected flees to Spain to fight against Franco. The novel deviates from Mary's memory of Lewis – Oliver returns from the Spanish War.

If you are ever to travel to the wilderness of Canada and the Northwestern Territories and trek eighty kilometres west from the small town of Whati, you will come across a blue mirror of a lake, barely rippled. At eight kilometres, the calm, ice cold waters are four times the length of the Olympic rowing course at Long Beach, Los Angeles. But when the sun is at the same height in the sky as it was when Jumbo and Lewis rowed triumphantly to victory, the waters – as they did in Los Angeles – gleam gold.

This is Clive Lake, named after the man who explored and mapped this beautiful but deserted Canadian wilderness.

Lewis's obituary in *The Times* concluded with the paragraph:

> 'Lewis Clive's many friends, whatever their political views, will not forget his inspiring courage, and will find some consolation in the knowledge that he died gallantly on the Ebro front in what he was convinced was a critical struggle to save democracy for Spain and ultimately for Europe.'

Water's Gleaming Gold

In September 1939, two days after Germany invaded Poland, the United Kingdom declared war on Germany.

It was now the turn of the three Edwards brothers – Jumbo, Sphinx and Oswald – to fight for democracy.

Chapter 14

United in Effort

A few months prior to the outbreak of the Second World War, Jumbo had been posted four hundred and twenty miles north of London to Scotland. His new airbase was at Donibristle on the Firth of Forth, just north of Edinburgh. This posting also came with a promotion to Squadron Leader.

Originally operating with grass runways, Donibristle airfield was provided with two more robust tarmac runways. It was from these runways that Squadron Leader Hugh Edwards would train the young pilots and navigators to prepare for what was fast becoming the dreaded inevitability of war.

Jumbo's main role was in teaching the RAF trainees the skills required to navigate, and he would take the airmen up into the Scottish skies in a variety of different military aircraft. Foremost amongst these planes was the Miles Mentor, a three-seat cabin monoplane for use in instrument training, radio training, and communications work during both day and night time. Other training missions were conducted in the Supermarine Walrus, a rather odd-looking but highly effective amphibious biplane used for reconnaissance; the Gloster Gladiator, the RAF's last biplane fighter aircraft; and the Fairey Swordfish, a biplane torpedo bomber.

Whenever he was granted leave, Jumbo would return to the family in London. By 1939, the family had now increased to four. On October 30th, 1937, Mike gave birth to their second son: David Cecil Richard Edwards. David's first and second names were in honour of Jumbo's older brothers. During the Summer months, Mike would travel up to Scotland with their two young sons for boating holidays at Aberdour or camping trips to the Cairngorms.

When time and work commitments allowed him to, Jumbo would enter flying competitions.

In May 1939, Jumbo was one of nineteen competitors in the London to Isle of Man race, flying his own Avro Avian biplane. The course was a direct route from Hatfield Aerodrome to Blackpool, and across the Irish Sea to the Isle of Man. The total distance was just over two hundred and fifty miles, involving a sea crossing of sixty three miles. A navy vessel and a lifeboat patrolled the sea as a precaution against any mishaps.

Once more, Jumbo was up against familiar faces in the race such as Captain Edgar Percival, Alex Henshaw and Geoffrey de Havilland. For this race Jumbo would have company. He brought along a fearless and intrepid passenger – Mike.

Unusually for Jumbo, the air race was uneventful – finishing in fifth place behind the winner Geoffrey de Havilland. Due to Mike's rather diminutive size, she struggled to see much of the scenery as it sped past underneath their aeroplane.

The London to Isle of Man race was a prelude to the weekend's Manx Air Rally, a race around the island. Jumbo was entered for the Tynwald, a race for those aeroplanes which were less powerful – under one hundred and twenty horsepower. With Mike once again braving the passenger seat in their Avro Baby, the aeroplanes took flight on the first of three laps around the Isle of Man. From the passenger seat, Mike glimpsed what she thought was an aeroplane floating in the sea off the west coast, near the village of Kirk Michael. It later transpired that one of the competitors, Mr S. Cummings, had ditched into the sea. In the newspaper report, Mr

Jumbo and Mike relaxing on the Isle of Man with the Avro Avian, 1939.

Cummings dramatically recalled how his Blackbird Bluebird lost power and nose-dived into the water. He fought his way sixty feet back up to the surface and swam around for half an hour before he was picked up by fishermen in their boat. Whilst this drama was unfolding, Jumbo and Mike sped past the finishing line to win. Mike was thrilled and she was soon clambering out of the passenger seat to lift the Tynwald Cup.

This was a fitting and triumphant end to Jumbo's air racing. The declaration of war at the beginning of September resulted in Jumbo's full attention centred on the training of new airmen and navigators. There was no more time for the frivolity of air races.

Over the previous four years, and ever since Adolf Hitler announced that he would rearm Germany in violation of the Treaty of Versailles, the RAF had started a major expansion with airfields and aircraft. From forty two squadrons with eight hundred aircraft in 1934, the RAF had impressively expanded to one hundred and fifty-seven squadrons and three thousand and seven hundred aircraft by the time that Jumbo was at Donibristle training aircrews.

Following the outbreak of war, the RAF fast-tracked the training of aircrew. This was not just within Britain but in other Commonwealth nations – approximately 167,000 men in all. The RAF also integrated

Mike, Jumbo and Sphinx on holiday in Scotland, Summer 1939.

Polish, Czech and other European airmen who had escaped from Hitler's Europe. Many of these new arrivals were now under the training of Jumbo, learning to fly and navigate mid-range bombers and fighters.

These newly recruited airmen would be assigned to one of the three major combat commands based in the UK. RAF Fighter Command was charged with defence of the country; RAF Bomber Command operated the bombers that would go on the offensive against the enemy; and RAF Coastal Command was to protect vital Allied shipping and supplies from attack by enemy shipping, especially the feared U-Boats.

In the first few months of the war, Germany still hoped to persuade Britain to reach a peace agreement. Although London hospitals prepared for 300,000 casualties in the first week, Germany unexpectedly did not immediately attack British cities by air. This inactivity lasted for several months and was dubbed the 'Phoney War'. During these fretful months the British Expeditionary Force (BEF) was sent to France to prepare for, and dissuade, a German invasion.

United in Effort

The Air Component of the BEF went to France to support the British and French Armies and within this Advanced Air Striking Force was 53 Squadron. Sphinx had been transferred to 53 Squadron and as Squadron Leader his flying skills were now required for vital and dangerous photographic reconnaissance duties over Germany. Sphinx flew several missions to monitor the build-up of airfields and industrial sites in the Rühr Valley.

On May 10th, 1940, the Phoney War ended abruptly. Germany launched air and ground attacks against Belgium and the Netherlands. This Blitzkrieg that had been so effective in Poland, combining tanks, infantry and artillery to devastate defences, now overwhelmed the Allied forces. With German forces invading France through the Ardennes, 53 Squadron had to quickly evacuate and by May 20th, Sphinx and his squadron were back in the south east of England. The role of reconnaissance was now supplemented with night time bombing, and 53 Squadron were incorporated into Coastal Command.

Up in Scotland, Jumbo was about to embark on his first wartime mission. The immediate need to train pilots was still the main priority of Jumbo's role with the RAF, but with the war now raging across the North Sea, Jumbo flew three missions in one week at the beginning of July.

The first two of these missions was piloting a Bristol Blenheim Mark IV, a compact bomber with the advantage of range over other fighter aircraft. The Blenheim could penetrate deep into enemy territory, making it ideal for reconnaissance duties. However, with a limited top speed, cumbersome to fly and slow in turning, the hope of all Blenheim aircrews was to avoid any encounter with enemy aircraft. On July 4th, with a navigator and a camera operator, Jumbo took off from Donibristle and set course for Molde on the Norwegian coast – a journey of nine hundred kilometres.

With Germany's invasion of Norway three months previously, it was imperative that reconnaissance was undertaken on the Norwegian naval bases. Jumbo's first mission was uneventful, and the crew returned to Scotland with their reconnaissance film ready to be developed and analysed.

Four days later, on the 8th, Jumbo was once again piloting a Blenheim to Norway. For this second reconnaissance mission he had to avoid German air defences and fly over the port town of Trondheim to provide photographic evidence on the positions of the German navy. Jumbo's aircrew managed to locate and photograph the fearsome German heavy cruiser, *Admiral Hipper*.

The success of Jumbo's mission confirmed to military intelligence that the *Admiral Hipper* was now at anchor in Trondheim, after landing troops in Norway during the German invasion in April. It was during this operation that the *Admiral Hipper* encountered the British destroyer HMS *Glowworm*. The German heavy cruiser severely crippled the *Glowworm* and – in the chaos of battle – the heavily damaged *Glowworm* rammed *Admiral Hipper*. The German heavy cruiser was only superficially damaged from the collision, but *Glowworm* sank beneath the waves with only thirty-one out of the *Glowworm's* complement of one hundred and forty nine being saved.

The day after his successful hunt for the *Admiral Hipper*, Jumbo's third mission was to pilot a Gloster Gladiator for a patrol over the Shetland Islands. The Gladiator was the RAF's last biplane fighter aircraft, and was beginning to be superseded with the development of the monoplane fighters, such as the Hurricane. However, the Gladiator was still in use in 1940 and remained an ideal option for a quick reconnaissance mission up north to the Shetlands.

After completing a busy week of reconnaissance and patrols, Jumbo flew himself down to London to see Mike and the children.

The family returned to Elsham Road, Kensington, to visit Jumbo's mother. Jumbo's sister, Mona, had recently been assigned by the Home Office to the internment camps on the Isle of Man. This was the location for several Alien Internment Camps during the war, and it was Mona's job as Deputy Camp Commandant to help with the administration of the women and children. She was concerned primarily with the general welfare and security for some four thousand internees, mainly young women, advising on education schemes and encouraging employment.

A few years previously, in 1932, Mona had been appointed as Guide and Lecturer at the Natural History Museum in London. The news of Mona's appointment made headlines. There was a novelty to the appointment as Mona was the first female to be appointed by the Trustees of the British Museum to the role of Guide and Lecturer.

The Vote, a newspaper established to support equal rights and the organ of the Women's Freedom League, excitedly reported Mona's recruitment on their front page. In the article, Mona explained that her chief qualification was a 'genuine interest in animals' – though she had also graduated from King's College London with an Honours degree in Zoology. Her role with the museum was to conduct parties or individuals around the various exhibits and to give information which would arouse interest. As *The Vote* explained, 'With no such guidance visitors are apt to wander aimlessly from gallery to gallery and derive little benefit from their visit'.

Sphinx had also managed to prise himself away from his duties at 53 Squadron and the brothers had a chance to reunite and talk about what they had experienced over the past few months. Sphinx had recently been promoted to Wing Commander of 53 Squadron, coordinating the operations of several squadrons. He was also flying missions, but the daytime aerial reconnaissance missions over Germany had now been replaced with adrenaline-inducing night time bombing raids.

One family member missing from the reunion was Oswald, Jumbo's younger brother. Oswald, who had joined the army after leaving University, had been deployed to Burma in 1938 as part of the Burma Frontier Force. Now promoted to Captain with the Myitkyina Battalion, Oswald wrote to his mother frequently whenever he had time away from patrolling the jungles and guarding the airfields on the air reinforcement route to Singapore.

At the end of the weekend, it was time for the family to part. Jumbo was to return to Scotland, Sphinx to RAF Detling in Kent, the base of 53 Squadron, and Mike and the boys to their cottage in Wiltshire – to where they had recently moved.

It was to be the last time that his family would see Sphinx.

On September 5th, in a news item headlined 'Noted Airman Missing', *The Scotsman* reported, 'Wing Commander E. C. T. Edwards, King's Cup Winner in 1931, and one of the first members of the Oxford University Air Squadron, is reported missing as a result of air missions last month'.

On hearing the alarming news of his brother, Jumbo was given permission to borrow a Percival Proctor – a single-engined monoplane used primarily for training purposes – to fly down from Scotland to Kent and find out what he could.

A few weeks earlier, RAF Detling had been on the receiving end of a daylight Luftwaffe raid – a day the Germans codenamed 'Adlertag' (Eagle Day). At least fifty German aircraft set out to bomb Detling and RAF Rochford. Twenty-two RAF aircraft were destroyed on the ground, the hangars were set alight and a direct hit on the operations room killed the commanding officer.

Flying a Proctor down to Kent was viewed as risky in the extreme – with its relative slow speed and lack of any machine guns, the Proctor would be defenceless against any enemy planes. The danger was of no consideration to Jumbo. It was imperative to discover what had happened to Sphinx.

Jumbo approached RAF Detling shortly after 15.30 hours. He was constantly scanning the skies for any sign of the Luftwaffe, who had made RAF Detling a priority target for constant raids. As he started his descent to the airstrip he was surprised by the lack of activity on the ground. Usually maintenance crews, and other servicemen, would be bustling around the aircraft and hangars.

Jumbo landed the Proctor and taxied towards one of the hangars. Again, he was puzzled as to why there were no personnel to greet his arrival. It was then that he could hear the wailing of an air siren. He switched off the engine and clambered out of the cockpit. Running towards him was a lone figure. The approaching figure was yelling, 'Get to cover. Get to cover'. The man grabbed Jumbo and raced with him to a slit trench adjacent to the runway. As the pair jumped into the trench the sound of several Messerschmitt Bf 109s split the air – then the crack of rapid machine gun fire. This was followed by the unmistakable engine noise of the Stuka, the feared German dive bomber and ground-attack aircraft.

As Jumbo recounted, 'Very soon the bombs were pouring down. It was a short sharp raid, with the ground beneath me reverberating with the "thump" of explosions. Though one felt perfectly safe in the slip trench, I was surprised to find a tree on fire only one hundred feet away. Thankfully the Proctor that I had borrowed from my base in Scotland was untouched by the machine guns and bombs of the Luftwaffe".

Once the air raid was over, Jumbo clambered out of the trench and made his way past burning wreckage and newly made craters to the operations room to meet with 53 Squadron. He needed to find out what he could about their Wing Commander – his brother Sphinx. Jumbo recounted the details from one of the airmen who was on the mission.

'Coastal Command had given 53 Squadron the duty of bombing the invasion ports, and in particular the concentration of barges building up all the way from the Maas to the Seine, the oil tanks and other small targets of strategic importance. On the night of August 31st Sphinx had taken on a mission for an evening raid on the Vlaardingen oil plant, a city in the south of Holland. Sphinx was piloting a Blenheim and with him was Sergeant Lionel Beesley and Sergeant Thomas Benjamin. The six Blenheims on the raid had to achieve a high degree of accuracy because there were only two squadrons employed on this raid, and the long nosed Blenheim could not carry many bombs. So night raids were ruled out. Accuracy demanded a low level attack; but the Blenheim was unsuitable for this. The tactics which Sphinx evolved were to fly in at dusk at a height of eight thousand feet, throttle back the engines at a distance of five miles from the target, and then to peel off into a steep dive and after steadying up in the dive with the sights dead on the target, release the bombs at a height of one thousand feet. Then, with urgency, break away and return to base, with the remaining Blenheims in loose formation astern, returning to Detling independently. This method gave little opportunity for the enemy flak gunner. On this particular occasion when set in the dive, Sphinx found he was not dead on the target, the oil tanks at Vlaardingen, so he aborted his bombing run and went round again. The second time the flak got him.'

Sphinx's Blenheim was catastrophically damaged from the flak. Sphinx had faced many emergencies in the air during missions and air races, and countless forced landings. But this time the damage was too crippling.

Trailing a dirty-grey wisp of smoke, the Blenheim banked sharply, turned back and dived for the second time into the flak that was now firing at full blast. In the middle of the bombing approach the machine was hit again and plummeted to the ground in flames.

The burning wreckage of the Blenheim impacted near the village of Pernis – onto farmland belonging to the van Galen family. The damage was such that there was no hope that Sphinx and his two crew could have survived.

Once it was safe to approach the twisted metal, the van Galen family tried to recover what personal effects they could. They buried the bodies amongst the grass and the forget-me-nots.

The villagers came to the graves and adorned them with flowers, which attracted the police. Any public demonstration of mourning for Allied crew had been forbidden by the occupying German forces, and within a few weeks the army arrived and removed the wreckage of the Blenheim. The Germans also took the remains of Sphinx, Beesley and Benjamin and reinterred them in a Rotterdam cemetery.

After the war, Jumbo visited the Netherlands to see where his brother was buried and to thank the van Galen family. In his notes he writes movingly of his visit:

'In the midst of the busy seaport and bustling city of Rotterdam there is an oasis of peace and quiet. Surrounded by a moat and bisected by a small canal there are fifty acres protected by pines, acacias, weeping willows trailing their branches in the water and by hedges which divide it up and give privacy. It is the cemetery of Begraafplaats Crooswijk. It is a lovely spot by nature, where art and industry have combined to make it more beautiful still.

If you go across the bridge and incline to the right, you come to the most beautiful spot of all in the North East corner. Here to mark it out as something special is a plinth surmounted by a stone cross carrying a sword, with two flagstaffs – one on either side. Amidst the flower beds is a stone marking the grave of my dear brother Wing Commander E. C. T. Edwards, M.A, Pilot, Royal Air Force, 31st August 1940. Alongside those of his Observer and of his Air Gunner: Sergeants Beesley and Benjamin.'

Jumbo stood in front of the grave of his brother. Killed at the age of thirty-five. Memories flooded back. Their childhood in Oxfordshire, their shared love of the river, the roar of the multitudes lining the banks of the Thames for the Boat Race, the cheers of the crowd as he sprinted across the grass towards Sphinx's aeroplane after he won the King's Cup. His brother, the inscrutable Sphinx.

It was a devastating loss.

Chapter 15

Night of the Thousand Bombers

In the same month as Jumbo's flying visit to RAF Detling, Oxford University Air Squadron (OUAS) was re-established. The OUAS had temporarily closed at the outbreak of war, but in September 1940 it was once again put into operation. This was the squadron that both Jumbo and Sphinx had joined as undergraduates, and where they had developed their flying skills. Sphinx had also been the first member of the OUAS to qualify as a pilot. Now, with the ongoing need for the RAF to recruit and train more airmen, the OUAS required a Commanding Officer. Jumbo had been contacted about the position and had applied. If successful it would mean that he would be back in Oxfordshire with Mike and their boys, and commanding a squadron to which he had an emotional tie.

In October 1940, Squadron Leader Hugh Edwards was appointed as the Commanding Officer. The OUAS was open to any Oxford undergraduate or graduate and was a training unit specialising in short courses for ground training to the standard of the RAF Initial Training School 'Wings' syllabus. Within the first month it had attracted almost one hundred members.

As opposed to taking part in any missions himself, Jumbo was once again concentrating fully on training young pilots and navigators, ensuring that they were fully prepared when transferred to squadrons and to fly missions.

Jumbo could also spend a lot more time with Mike and the family, allowing him to recover emotionally from the loss of his brother. News of Sphinx's death had also been communicated to the Far East where Jumbo's younger brother, Oswald, was still enduring the seasonal monsoon rains in the jungles of Burma.

At the start of the war the RAF had no real means of determining the success of its operations. Crews would return with only their word as to the amount of damage that had been inflicted, or even if they had bombed the target. The Butt Report, commissioned by the Government and released in August 1941, revealed the widespread failure of bombing missions. The conclusion was that only about one-third of aircraft claiming to reach their target actually achieved this aim. There was a desperate need to address this shortcoming and to ensure an improvement in the standards of navigation. Consequently, further air observer schools were established. One of these was on the Isle of Man.

RAF Jurby, located on the west coast of the Isle of Man, reverted to its former title of No. 5 Air Observer School. The teaching of navigation, bomb aiming and air gunnery now formed a considerable part of the station's remit.

As part of the reorganisation, Handley Page Hampden aircraft arrived at Jurby – joining the Avro Ansons and the other training aircraft. Instructors were screened personnel who had all completed operations and who had a wealth of experience in navigation. Jumbo was identified as an ideal candidate to train crews in the art and technique of navigating.

He once again said farewell to Mike and the boys and travelled to the Isle of Man to take up his new position. He knew RAF Jurby fairly well, having raced his aeroplane over the airfield in the Manx Air Rally. His sister, Mona, was also on the island as one of the Deputy Camp Commandants for the Alien Internment Camps.

The training would take part in the classrooms and in the air, navigating a Hampden out over the North Atlantic and practising bombing runs on outcrops of rock, such as Rockall, an uninhabitable granite islet. The Hampden itself was conceived as a fast, manoeuvrable 'fighting bomber', with a crew of four: a pilot, navigator/bomb aimer, radio operator and rear gunner. It was often referred to by aircrews as the 'Flying Suitcase' because of its cramped crew conditions, being wide enough only for a single person. The navigator sat behind the pilot and, once in place, the crew had almost no room to move. 'A beautiful aeroplane to fly, terrible to fly in' was a constant refrain by those who were now training within the confines of this bomber.

Although the Hampden was designed with speed and agility in mind – and ideal for training purposes – they were quickly outclassed by German fighters such as the Messerschmitt. This was tragically exposed during early daytime bombing campaigns above enemy territory. As a result, the Hampden's role turned into specialised night bombing, but even so, the casualty rate for Hampden bombers was still high. The playful sobriquet of the 'flying suitcase' remained but by the Summer of 1942 the Hampdens were being replaced by the more spacious Vickers Wellington, and the more powerful four-engined Avro Lancaster.

Another consequence of the Butt Report was the appointment of Arthur Harris as Commander-in-Chief of Bomber Command in February 1942. 'Bomber' Harris was a proponent of the belief that massive and sustained aerial bombing alone would force Germany to surrender. In the Summer of 1942, whilst Jumbo was continuing to train the aircrews, Harris and Bomber Command received the go-ahead for a massive demonstration of the RAF's power – the 'thousand bomber raid'.

The term 'thousand bomber raid' was a propaganda device, used to fire the imagination of the British public. Bomber Command attempted to reach the fabled thousand number of bombers by including not only bombers that were currently operational as part of RAF Bomber Command, but also aircrews from Operational Training Units. RAF Jurby was

The Handley Page Hampden, 1942. It quickly gained the nickname of 'The Flying Suitcase'.

contacted and a request for pilots and bombers was made by Bomber Command. The Commanding Officer offered up the use of five Hampdens and aircrews to participate in the bombing raids.

For Jumbo, this was madness. The Hampdens of RAF Jurby were not up to the job of flying a mission over to Germany, especially towards the heavily defended Rühr Valley. The five Hampdens were used exclusively for training purposes and as such the aircraft had been flown for short periods involving frequent starting and taxiing over a sandy airfield. Jumbo's fears were that this would affect the long-range capability and reliability of the aircraft and that by agreeing to release the crews it would put their lives in even greater danger.

Jumbo made this point clear to the Commanding Officer, but the demand for a thousand bombers required all units to contribute to the mission.

Jumbo – as with most Squadron Leaders – had a fundamental rule. He would never ask an airman to pilot or navigate an aeroplane that he was unwilling to fly. So he put himself forward to pilot one of the Hampdens for the mission.

Rather surprisingly, he had never written a will. But now, as a husband and father, he quickly scrawled out his will and posted it to his mother in London. Along with the will, his letter detailed that he was about to embark on a mission that was, in his mind, an act of folly but to 'not worry'.

The five Hampdens took off from RAF Jurby on May 26th and headed to RAF Syerston in Nottinghamshire.

The next two days were spent making the aircraft operational. This included fitting balloon cable cutters, bomb racks and other armament.

Jumbo and his air crew discovered that they were to fly in the second of the 'thousand bomber' missions – a raid over Essen.

On the second day of air-testing at Syerston, it was discovered that the Hampdens that Jumbo had brought over from RAF Jurby had excessive oil consumption due to the extensive use of the aircraft in short practice take-offs. This was exactly what Jumbo had feared. The aircraft were deemed as unsuitable for the mission out to Essen and back. As a replacement, Jumbo was provided with one Hampden from 408 Squadron.

On the evening of June 1st, the day of the mission, Jumbo sat down at his desk. In his neat, spidery handwriting, he scribbled out a few lines from Robert Browning's poem *Prospice*:

I was ever a fighter, so – one fight more,
The best and the last!
I would hate that death bandaged my eyes and forbore,
And bade me creep past.

The short excerpt, and the cream-coloured slip of paper on which it was scrawled, was placed carefully inside his logbook. If this was to be his last fight, then so be it.

Shortly before midnight, Jumbo taxied his borrowed Hampden onto the airstrip at Syerston and powered up the engines for take-off.

Jumbo had hand-picked his crew from RAF Jurby, and selected those that he had trained and had the utmost trust in. For the mission to be a success he had to rely on the very best, and they had to rely on him. As with the coxless four, each crew member in the Hampden had his specific role. Success in a mission would be a combined team effort. His navigator/bomb aimer was Flight Sergeant Hamilton, Flight Officer Smith was the radio operator and Flight Officer Brown took up the rear gunner position within the narrow confines of the 'flying suitcase'.

In total there were nine hundred and fifty-six bombers that were heading from airfields throughout the UK and towards the Rühr Valley and

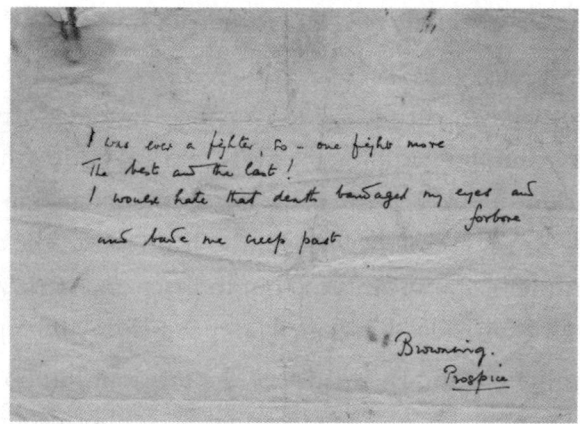

Excerpt from 'Prospero' that Jumbo scribbled out before his mission to Essen. He would keep this scrap of paper in his logbook.

the industrial town of Essen. Jumbo's Hampden was in a tight formation with the other Hampdens from RAF Syerston and they had the comfort of an escort of fighter planes to ensure safe passage across the North Sea. As soon as they approached the Dutch coastline they were on their own.

The hope was that the Hampden formation would have timed their raid to coincide with a cloudless night above their target of the Krupp steelworks. However, military intelligence briefs warned that there was usually a persistent haze of smog due to the heavy industry in and around the target.

Shortly before 01.00 hours, the first bombers reached Essen. Wellingtons from No. 3 Group led the raid, their role to identify the target by dropping flares. The second wave consisted of one hundred and twenty-five heavy bombers laden with incendiary bombs. The RAF pilots of these heavy bombers soon realised that the target area was not only obscured by the industrial haze, but that there was a layer of cloud. The weather had not been kind. As a result, a lot of the flares that had been dropped by the Wellingtons had been inaccurate and had missed lighting up the primary target of the Krupp factories.

Night of the Thousand Bombers

Following behind the heavy bombers were the vast majority of the RAF planes. Amongst this third wave was Jumbo piloting his Hampden. The time was shortly before 02.00 hours and Jumbo and the crew had navigated the plane to perfection – they were ten miles from their target.

The night sky ahead of them was beginning to be lit by flak that shot through the clouds and haze towards the formation of approaching bombers. The crew had forgotten about their discomfort and were now concentrating fully on preparing the Hampden for the bombing raid.

The sky was alive with explosions and bursting shells. The crew could feel the reverberation, the thump, thump of the shells as they exploded above and below. The cloud was providing cover for the Hampden, but it was also obscuring the intended target. Suddenly, and alarmingly, Jumbo felt the Hampden lurch. The port engine had cut out. The fear was that they had been hit by flak, but there was no visual sign of damage or any catastrophic loss of control.

Desperately, Jumbo tried to restart the engine. The port engine spluttered back into life.

He now had a decision to make – a momentous decision for all of his crew. Jumbo could abandon the bombing raid and put his Hampden into a sharp bank to return to England, or he could carry on to the intended target of the Krupp steelworks and drop his incendiary bombs to complete the mission. Jumbo took the decision to proceed with the bombing run. He prayed that the port engine would not stall again.

The flak and anti-aircraft fire was even heavier now as the Hampden started on the approach to the target. The navigator, Flight Sergeant Hamilton, yelled out directions as Jumbo fought to keep the Hampden level and on course. A sudden break in the clouds revealed the looming bulk of the steelworks beneath them. Hamilton yelled from his position behind the cockpit, 'Bombs away!'.

Jumbo operated the switch to drop the 1,600 lb of incendiary bombs. The Hampden leapt up as the weight of the bomb load was released.

The cluster of incendiaries rained down, detonating in the railway yard adjoining the steelworks. Jumbo immediately put the Hampden into a steep bank, desperate to get away from the anti-aircraft fire. The port engine cut out.

The Hampden was now flying with just the one engine, and the flak was still exploding around them. Jumbo had to wrestle with the controls, taking violent evasive action as shell after shell detonated – the plane reverberating with the shockwaves.

With immense nerve and skill, Jumbo piloted the plane out of the hell of the Essen skies. The flak ceased, but the port engine was not responding to Jumbo's desperate attempts to restart it. He would have to fly the aircraft back to England on one engine, traversing over a hundred miles of enemy territory before reaching the North Sea.

The Hampden had lost considerable speed and was now on its own. There was to be no safety in numbers. Jumbo and Flight Sergeant Hamilton plotted out a course that would take them over German and Dutch territory, avoiding any major towns or cities. Their desperate hope was to avoid the fast, and heavily armed, enemy fighters that had been scrambled to intercept the returning bombers.

Sergeant Brown, in the rear gunner position, constantly scanned the night skies above and behind them, but he was fully aware that if any enemy plane was to find them then it would make short work of the crippled Hampden. There was also the fear that dawn would soon break and the darkness that was aiding their escape would fade away into a crystal clear Summer morning.

Jumbo spotted the coastline of Holland as daylight began to seep across the landscape below. Soon they were above the North Sea and the crew began to relax slightly and to think about home.

With a jolting shudder, the Hampden lurched again and began to lose height. Jumbo managed to level the plane out, but they were now perilously close to the sea – flying at four hundred feet. Jumbo shouted out orders to the crew. They needed to jettison anything that they could – ammunition, equipment, anything that could be thrown out of the aircraft. Despite the cramped interior of the Hampden, the crew were now fully concentrated on keeping the plane from ditching. There was no option to bail out at this height. Jumbo nursed the plane towards land, praying that the starboard engine would not fail.

There was no hope of returning to Nottinghamshire, but the nearest English coastline was Norfolk and Jumbo kept on a steady course towards safety. Shortly before 06.00 hours, Jumbo spotted the welcome beaches of the Norfolk coast. As the Hampden struggled its way towards the coastline and Jumbo noticed in the distance an aerodrome that was under construction.

As he flipped the switch for the undercarriage to be deployed the starboard engine finally gave out.

Jumbo was now at the controls of a Hampden bomber that had lost all power to its engines.

He would have to glide the plane towards the fast approaching, and newly constructed, grass airstrip. Memories of grappling with his Baby Avro as he crash landed into the field outside of Warrington flashed through his mind, but he kept calm. The Hampden swept down onto the airstrip and juddered to a halt.

The four crew sat in silence for a moment, as maintenance workers raced towards the plane. They had survived. Somehow.

The raid on Essen was not classified as a success, despite the loss of only thirty-one aircraft. The cloud cover had prevented any meaningful accuracy from the bombers. Heavy damage was done in neighbouring towns, notably Oberhausen and Mülheim, but Essen itself escaped lightly and Krupp steelworks was almost untouched from the bombs. However, there was one Hampden that had made it through to the target and had dropped its incendiaries with accuracy. That it did so and made a successful return to England on one engine was a true mark of the excellence and bravery of its air crew.

For the 'act of exemplary gallantry while flying', Squadron Leader Hugh Edwards was awarded the Air Force Cross.

For Jumbo's family there was just relief that he was back home, though this joy would turn once more to despair. A letter received at the house in Kensington informed Jumbo's mother that her youngest son, Captain Oswald Edwards, was missing in action.

While commanding a column in the jungles of Burma, Oswald was ambushed by Japanese forces south of the city of Prome. Oswald's body was never recovered. Anne Edwards had lost another son. Jumbo and Mona another brother.

There was only a week of recuperation with Mike and the boys before Jumbo was back on the Isle of Man and teaching the young pilots and navigators, preparing them for missions yet to come.

Chapter 16
Crash Positions

The Handley Page Hampden was withdrawn from service as an active bomber. Its limited defensive capabilities had persuaded the RAF that it was too much of a risk to the aircrews on missions over heavily defended targets. It still remained as an excellent aircraft for training purposes, but Jumbo was now training his aircrew in the Blenheim, which had proved itself more effective as a bomber.

By the beginning of 1943 there were signs that the Allies were starting to turn the tide of war against the Axis. The German and Italian forces were on the retreat in North Africa, the United States was now actively fighting in Europe – with the first bombing raids on Italy in December 1942 – and in the Battle of the Barents Sea, the British won a strategic victory over the Germans. This naval defeat led Hitler to scrap the surface fleet and order the German Navy to concentrate on U-boat warfare.

In February 1943, 53 Squadron required a new Wing Commander. The squadron that was previously led by Sphinx was now based at RAF Docking in Norfolk. As part of Coastal Command, 53 Squadron was primarily involved in maritime reconnaissance. There was an emotional tie with 53 Squadron for Jumbo, and he knew many of the Squadron Leaders through their friendship and respect for Sphinx. Jumbo applied for a transfer from RAF Jurby to 53 Squadron and in February he was promoted to Wing Commander. He had succeeded his brother and took up his new position at RAF Docking.

As Wing Commander, Jumbo's main responsibility was coordinating the operations of the squadron – he was also back flying training missions. Coastal Command had just taken delivery from the United States a new long-range aircraft: the Consolidated B-24 Liberator. The high cruise speed, long range and heavy bomb load made the Liberator an ideal plane for operating over the Atlantic for U-boat hunting and convoy escort duty. The German U-boat menace was sinking thousands of tons of shipping in the mid-Atlantic area, where air cover for convoys was absent, and so the need for the Liberator was of paramount importance.

Jumbo took an immediate liking to the Liberator. It was responsive to fly and far more spacious than the Hampden or Blenheim. The Liberator carried a crew of up to ten. A typical layout had the pilot and co-pilot alongside each other in a well-glazed cockpit. The navigator and bombardier sat in the 'greenhouse' nose with two flexible ball-mounts built into it for forward defensive firepower. The radio/radar operator sat behind the pilots, facing sideways and sometimes doubling as a waist gunner. The flight engineer was positioned adjacent to the radio operator behind the pilots; he operated the upper gun turret, located just behind the cockpit and in front of the wing.

After a few months putting the Liberator through its paces, 53 Squadron were on the move and redeployed to the South Coast of England. RAF Thorney Island, seven miles east of Portsmouth, provided a base to commence the long-range patrols and Atlantic convoy escorts that the Liberator was intended for.

In the Summer of 1943, 53 Squadron used these South Coast bases to participate in Operation Musketry, an RAF operation over the Bay of Biscay instigated to find and destroy U-boats running on the surface while on transit to or from their hunting areas in the Atlantic. During July and August, three times a day, seven aircraft flew parallel courses after reaching an area off Cape Finisterre in neutral Spain. When a U-boat was sighted and reported, the aircraft then converged and attacked as a pack. The tactic proved to be very effective, and the Liberators of 53 Squadron joined several other squadrons on the long-range patrols.

Jumbo was determined to be an active Wing Commander, one who participated in the missions, and assigned himself to eight Musketry patrols. On August 11th, Jumbo was on patrol and approaching the north-western coastline of Spain.

The weather conditions were perfect, and the Bay of Biscay below him was calm. He sighted a submarine that had surfaced and was now making its way towards the Galician port and city of Ferrol. This was the perfect time to put the Liberator through its paces, and to go on the attack. As Jumbo prepared the crew for an attack, the navigator suddenly informed Jumbo that he had identified the submarine as 'similar in silhouette and colour to a Spanish C-2'.

Spain was nominally neutral during the war, though under General Franco's far-right Nationalist regime it was politically aligned with Nazi Germany. It was an open secret that German U-boats were utilising Spanish ports for resupplies and repairs.

Jumbo had a decision to make. He informed the crew to continue to prepare for an attack run. If anything, it would provide ideal practice for when they encountered German U-boats.

He circled around and brought his Liberator down to one hundred feet and made an approach towards the Spanish submarine. With visibility so good, the Spanish submariners had seen the Liberator circling above and start to descend towards them. They rushed to the anti-aircraft guns.

Although Jumbo's logbook does not make it clear if the submarine fired first, Jumbo released eight depth charges and banked quickly to avoid the incoming fire. The depth charges exploded with two mighty plumes of water four hundred yards in front of the Spanish submarine. The rear gunner also shot two hundred rounds at the U-Boat. Jumbo called off

Consolidated B-24 Liberator of 53 Squadron
© *Doug Harrington*

the attack, and gained altitude to observe the submarine make its rapid escape into the safety of Ferrol harbour.

The depth charging of the Spanish submarine gave his crew invaluable experience of a daytime attack. It also provided Jumbo with a sense of satisfaction that he had fought back against Franco – in remembrance of his friend, Lewis Clive.

The Spanish Government were not so enamoured of a Liberator attacking one of their submarines and it caused a diplomatic issue between the Governments. However, as the Liberator had been fired upon, Jumbo was only given a stern word of warning to avoid such encounters in the future. Captain Peyton Ward – Naval Liaison Officer to RAF Coastal Command – concluded the official report with the comment, 'No damage. I admire the frank remarks by the Squadron Commander and glad the experience so gained was only at the expense of a Spanish submarine.'

The patrols over the Bay of Biscay continued throughout the Summer. Operation Musketry was followed by Operation Percussion – which once again involved Liberators from 53 Squadron. Percussion was specific to hunting down and destroying German U-boats attempting to leave or reach French ports by means of a surface transit of the Bay of Biscay.

In the early hours of September 17th, Jumbo had taken off in his Liberator and set a course for the Bay of Biscay for a routine patrol as part of Operation Percussion. Three hours later, at 05.00 hours, a message was received from Base for Wing Commander Edwards to divert and 'to position 4520/1108 and make square search for dinghy. Catalina in contact'.

The previous day, at 16.30 hours, a Sunderland – a flying boat patrol bomber – had radioed to Base, 'Being attacked by enemy aircraft'. Then silence. The Sunderland from 461 Squadron, a Royal Australian

Air Force maritime patrol squadron, had been patrolling over the Bay of Biscay when it was intercepted by six Junker Ju88s. The Australian crew of the Sunderland fought bravely for forty minutes but the combined firepower of six enemy aircraft was too much to defend against and the captain, Flight Lieutenant Dudley Marrows, successfully ditched his badly damaged Sutherland into the ocean. The eleven aircrew managed to inflate two dinghies and drifted away from the fast sinking Sunderland. One of the dinghies rapidly deflated from shrapnel damage, and so the air crew had to clamber into the one inflated dinghy. As Marrows recalled, 'Eleven men, one painfully wounded, sitting in the dinghy, legs inward, like the petals of a closely petalled flower'.

The dinghy drifted like this throughout the night but then they heard the sound of an aircraft engine.

'We used the one remaining distress rocket. The aircraft was one of ours – a Catalina, a Leigh light-equipped flying boat. They made an approach on us and there we were lit up by a bloody wonderful great searchlight. They dropped markers, sent off appropriate signals and signalled to us that help was on the way. It then flew off, having reached its limit of fuel endurance.'

Jumbo's instructions were to rendezvous above the location of the dinghy, as signalled by the Catalina, and to oversee the rescue of the Australians by ship.

The Catalina had not long disappeared when Marrows, with immense relief, spotted Jumbo's Liberator above them. However, it became apparent that the Liberator was unable to spot their small dinghy. All of the marine markers that the Catalina had dropped had burnt out and the Liberator continued to circle and search for the Australians. There was much frustration and frantic waving of arms. The Australians could see the Liberator, but it could not see them. But Marrows had one last hope. He had kept his marine marker. They ignited the marker and tossed it clear of the dinghy. In a few heart-stopping moments it was trailing red flame and smoke for all to see. The Liberator came diving towards them.

The Australian aircrew standing in front of their dinghy after their dramatic Atlantic rescue, overseen by Jumbo and his crew © Marilyn Marrows Voullaire.

At 08.55 hours, Jumbo radioed back to Base: 'Over dinghy in position 4535/1210, with eleven live bodies'. By 10.00 hours, Jumbo had directed three Navy sloops to their location and radioed the good news that the Australians had been rescued.

A few weeks after his rescue, Dudley Matthews was interviewed by the BBC about their adventures and thanked the aircrews of the Catalina and the Liberator for saving their lives.

The patrols over the Bay of Biscay were always fraught with danger. The Germans would use their bases in France to ensure that they could protect and cover the U-boat transit routes, and hunt down the RAF aircraft.

Two weeks after Jumbo's search and rescue mission, he lost one of his aircrews, Flight Lieutenant John Rintoul and his crew of seven. A message was received at Base that they were being attacked by four enemy aircraft. A Liberator from 224 Squadron later reported seeing Rintoul's plane being shot down into the sea. There were no survivors.

Since February 1943 when Jumbo took over Command, 53 Squadron had lost seven Liberators to enemy action or accidents and with this thirty-five airmen, with seven captured by the Germans. The number of lives they had saved by hunting and destroying U-boats was incalculable, but each missing airman was a devastating blow to all of the Squadron.

Even though RAF Beaulieu remained the main airbase of 53 Squadron, the Liberators would often fly out from RAF St Eval, on the North Cornish coast. This allowed the aircraft a shorter route to the Atlantic and out over the Bay of Biscay.

The 53 Squadron 'Score Board' with Wing Commander Edwards credited with saving eleven lives.

During October, the Squadron's Liberators were fitted with Leigh lights. This powerful light was the invention of Humphrey Leigh, a staff officer at HQ Coastal Command. A carbon-arc lamp was mounted beneath the starboard wing and for the first time it became possible to illuminate U-boats on the surface at night. Needless to say, it also gave the U-boats an excellent target to aim back at.

On Saturday, November 20th, eight Liberators of 53 Squadron took off from RAF St Eval airbase for a destination in the North Atlantic. The mission was to rendezvous with a large convoy of sixty-six Allied ships, escorted by twenty warships, that was carrying vital supplies of food, equipment and raw materials from Port Said via Gibraltar to the UK.

Jumbo allocated Liberator BZ819 to his command, a plane that he had flown several times down to the Bay of Biscay.

In mid-afternoon, Squadron Leader K. A. Aldridge was the first to take-off from St Eval in his Liberator BZ816. This was followed by a further six Liberators at regular time intervals. Finally, at 23.12 hours, Liberator BZ819 took to the night sky. On board the Liberator piloted by Jumbo was a crew that he had personally chosen as the 'best-of-the-best'. The crew were: Flight Officer Alexander Davis (co-pilot); Flight Lieutenant

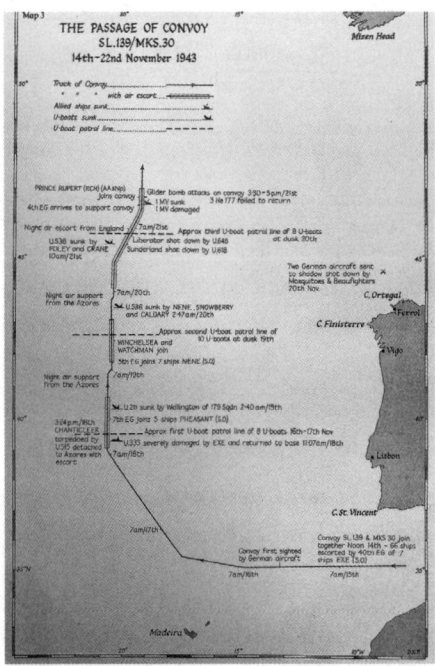

The route of Convoy SL139 from Gibraltar to the UK, November 1943.

Francis Halliday (navigator) of Toronto, Canada; Flight Lieutenant Bruce Hamilton (radio operator and gunner); Sergeant Stanley Johnson (flight engineer); Flight Sergeant William Owen (gunner); Warrant Officer George Shield (gunner) and; Sergeant Leonard Terry (gunner). The average age of Jumbo's crew was twenty-two. It had also not escaped his notice that he was in a crew of eight. With the London Rowing Club eight he was part of a perfect crew that had rowed to victory at Henley. The boys on the water were now his boys in the sky.

The escort mission to protect Convoy SL139 would be a round trip of approximately fifteen hundred miles for the Liberators. Carrying up to two and a half thousand gallons of fuel, the modified Liberator had an impressive range – about three hours of patrol time after flying a thousand miles from its base.

The Allied convoy had been spotted by the German Luftwaffe as soon as it had entered the Atlantic from the Mediterranean. As a consequence, it was being shadowed by a U-boat wolfpack. By the late evening of the 20th, the convoy had reached a point approximately six hundred and twenty miles due west from the north-west tip of Spain. The Liberators of 53 Squadron made radio contact with the convoy and in the early hours of the 21st the massed collection of Allied ships reported the comforting sight of the escort planes a few hundred feet above them.

At 04.00 hours on the morning of the 21st, the crew of BZ819 obtained a radar contact on one of the U-boats that had surfaced close to the convoy. The heart of the Liberator's anti-submarine capabilities was its microwave radar equipment, known as the Airborne Surface Vessel Detection ten-millimetre (ASV-10) radar. A skilful operator could identify a surfaced submarine at more than forty miles and a conning tower at fifteen to twenty miles.

Jumbo brought the Liberator down to fifty feet above the ink-black expanse of the Atlantic. When the plane had reached the limits of the radar, and a kilometre from the target, the order was made to switch on the Leigh light. This 22-million candlepower spotlight lit up the churning ocean. In the distance the outline of the 220-foot U-648 was detected.

The illuminated U-boat was now aware of the approach of the Liberator and under the command of Leutnant zur See Peter-Arthur Stahl the German crew were quick to man the anti-aircraft gun.

A few hours previously, and unknown to Jumbo, Squadron Leader Aldridge had also identified U-648 with his Leigh light equipped Liberator. Aldridge's aircraft had already performed one attack run towards the U-boat and coming around for a second run his Liberator was hit by fire from a quadruple 20 mm anti-aircraft gun. Aldridge's Liberator, in a trail of fire and smoke, plunged into the ocean. All nine crewmen were lost.

Jumbo continued to guide his plane towards the U-boat when tracer fire from the upper turret of the Liberator temporarily blinded him. Simultaneously, the U-boat opened fire from its anti-aircraft gun. Jumbo yelled to the bombardier to release the depth charges and then pulled back desperately on the yoke, whilst putting the plane into full throttle. As the Liberator thundered up and away from the U-boat the depth charges exploded at a depth of twenty-five metres.

The depth charges were not accurate enough to cause significant damage to Stahl's vessel. The U-boat retreated quickly back under the waves, and the Liberator returned to the Allied convoy.

Not long after this return to the skies above the convoy, the Liberator picked up a further radar contact.

Once more the crew prepared to attack another of the surfaced wolf-pack. Jumbo brought the plane down to fifty feet and this time the U-boat that was targeted was U-967, commandeered by Oberleutnant zur See Herbert Loeder. Jumbo issued the command to switch on the Leigh light and ready the depth charges. The spotlight failed to switch on.

The Liberator had been damaged by the anti-aircraft fire from the previous encounter. Without the spotlight illuminating the darkness there was nothing the Liberator could do other than to abort the attack and return to escort duty.

At 08.00 hours – as weak Winter daylight began to filter through the thick cloud cover – Jumbo left the convoy and the navigator, Frank Halliday, plotted a course due northeast to return to England. The fuel level was sufficient to fly the seven hundred miles back to RAF St Eval but as with all these Atlantic missions the plane would be returning with very little fuel left in the tanks.

It was a cold, grey, November day. With the low cloud level Jumbo had to fly a few hundred feet from the tops of the Atlantic waves to ensure that there was sufficient visibility. This would also avoid any chance encounter with enemy aircraft.

Six hours into the return flight, and only twenty miles from reaching base at St Eval, Alex Davies left his co-pilot seat and clambered down to the bomb bay. A decision had been made to transfer fuel from an auxiliary tank to the main fuel tanks. The crew began to flip the fuel switches to manage the flow.

Almost at once, the Liberator shuddered violently.

Three of the four engines ceased working, though the propellers kept rotating in the headwind. With an altitude of only three hundred feet there was no time at all to make any desperate attempt to restart the engines. At a speed of 120 mph, the seventeen-tonne Liberator went into a lurching nosedive towards the ocean. Crucially there was also no time to reduce the speed and lower the flaps, no time to issue a distress signal, no time to pull the lever in the fuselage that would automatically inflate and jettison the life rafts.

All that there was time for was one frantic yelled command from Jumbo: 'Crash positions'.

The Liberator had gained the ominous nickname of the 'flying coffin' both for its rather rectangular looks and, more darkly, for its limited options of exiting the plane in the event of a crash. The RAF had gathered statistics on the Liberator and its performance in a sea ditching: two-thirds of the planes broke up on impact.

Although it was only a matter of seconds before Liberator BZ819 was to hit the Atlantic, the term 'flying coffin' would have crossed the panicked minds of the eight-man crew.

The Liberator hit the ocean nose first. The plane snapped in two with the rear portion of the fuselage breaking off aft of the bomb bay. The windscreen shattered instantaneously, and a surge of freezing cold seawater swept into the cockpit.

The tumultuous noise of shattered metal and machinery was quickly replaced by silence. Without a sealed fuselage, a Liberator would sink within a minute. Miraculously, the front portion of the Liberator was still floating on top of the waves – buoyancy provided by the wings that were still attached.

It would surely be only a matter of minutes, if not seconds, before the ocean would claim the entirety of the plane. Jumbo managed to release his seat belt and desperately clambered through the smashed frame of the cockpit and up onto the top side of the plane. Bloodied, soaking and panicked, the only instinct was to get out. Wearing heavy flying jackets and multiple layers, the Atlantic would soon drag them down. The crew were wearing 'Mae West' lifejackets, but these required the wearer to release a valve to inflate the lifejacket.

Jumbo emerged onto the top of the fuselage just as the rear section sank below the waves. There had been no time to pull the internal overhead lever to release and inflate the two life rafts. Jumbo would have to deploy the life rafts manually. This involved turning the raft-release levers located on the top of the fuselage and then clambering to the wings to free the now exposed life rafts from their cradles. This was a difficult enough manoeuvre when practised on a Liberator parked up on a runway, but now this vital task had to be completed on a barely buoyant plane with waves sweeping over the slippery metal of the broken fuselage.

As Jumbo frantically made his way to the release levers, he was aware that three of his crew had made it out of the gaping hole that was once the cockpit: Bruce Hamilton, William Owen and George Shield. They were all bloodied and injured, clinging to the plane and unable to assist. Their only hope was with their Wing Commander and the successful deployment of the life rafts.

As Jumbo reached the lever his mind was trying to recall the complicated instructions that were held within his well-thumbed operator's manual:

> 'LIFE RAFTS. Two Type A-2 life rafts are carried in the fuselage above the wing between Stations 4.2 and 4.4. To release either raft from inside the airplane, pull the "T" handle at the centre of the airplane on the upper part of the forward face of bulkhead at Station 4.0. On B-240 No. 41-23640 and on, the "T" handle is located immediately aft of the top escape hatch. The pull cable releases the lock pins holding the life raft doors closed and allows the spring bungee to throw the raft out, clear of the fuselage.
>
> A rip cord attached to the raft cradle automatically opens the valve which controls the raft inflation from the CO_2 bottle. To release either raft from outside the airplane, the lever flush in the fuselage aft of each door should be lifted up and twisted 90 degrees. This action pulls the same cable that attaches to the 'T' handle on the inside and releases the raft in the same manner as described above. Do not release rafts until plane is at rest in the water.'

Jumbo reached the first lever. At any moment, with the ocean continuing to rush into the broken fuselage, the plane was sure to sink.

The freezing ocean water continued to pound over the stricken Liberator but, with immense difficulty, he lifted and rotated the lever. The door to the life raft cradle sprung open. But that was all. The life raft remained in the cradle uninflated.

Frantically, Jumbo manoeuvred himself towards the location of the second release lever. Once more the release lever was located and with hands numbed by the freezing water the lever was turned. This was the last chance for survival. The second cradle sprung open. The life raft, as with the first, remained uninflated.

The damage caused by the violent ditching was preventing the spring bungee from releasing the raft. With one final effort, Jumbo pulled desperately on the trapped life raft. With more of a whimper than the expected explosion, the life raft emerged from its cradle but without the energy required for the CO_2 canister to work fully – it only partially inflated the rubber cavity. However, it offered hope.

Relying on his pilot training and a memory of the manual instructions, Jumbo pulled with what strength he had remaining on the rip cord. A further release of carbon dioxide provided some additional inflation to the life raft, but it was not sufficient for any kind of buoyancy. There was only one further means of inflating the life raft and this was a top-up valve to which a hand operated concertina-type inflation bellows could be attached. Jumbo located the bellows and managed to attach them to the valve. He had only a matter of minutes before the Liberator would disappear for good.

Working desperately, Jumbo could only hope that his three crew would be able to cling on to the fuselage.

It would take a further five minutes before the life raft could be inflated enough to provide any kind of sea worthiness. With the life raft now fully rigged, and with Jumbo near to total exhaustion, he turned back to help his injured crew into the raft.

They were not there.

All that could be seen on the waves surrounding the stricken wreckage was a growing patch of black oil. Jumbo yelled out but there was to be no reply, no cries of help.

Jumbo clambered into the life raft just as the front portion of the Liberator sank, serenely, into the depths of the Atlantic. He manoeuvred the life raft in circles, calling out and frantically looking for any of his crew in the hope that they had managed to inflate their Mae Wests. By this time, what light there was had faded away. His crew, his friends, had gone. In this despair it was only then that the agonising pain of his injuries hit home. Jumbo had suffered five broken ribs and a collapsed lung.

With no further options available, Wing Commander Edwards – double Olympic champion and Oxford Blue – looked at the compass and took a bearing.

He began to row east.

Chapter 17

Rowing for Survival

It was common knowledge amongst the Coastal Command aircrew that the chances of surviving the Atlantic in an inflatable life raft – assuming one made a successful ditching – were, at best, slim. By the end of hostilities, 53 Squadron had lost a total of thirteen Liberators, one hundred and seven men, in incidents of ditching at sea.

Apart from Jumbo, none of the aircrews had survived. In fact, only two bodies had ever been accounted for – one washed up on the shoreline of France, the other in Spain. Regarding the particular area of the Atlantic that Liberator BZ819 ditched in, seventeen Allied aircraft came down within a seventy-mile vicinity of the Scilly Isles. Of these seventeen aircraft, eighty-three crew members were lost. The odds of survival were very grim.

Within the life raft, Jumbo had very limited supplies or equipment. A typical life raft would be stocked with the aluminium oars and some had a basic sail and mast. Alongside these rudimentary navigation aids were a few cans of fresh water, chocolate, a puncture repair kit, compass, the pump that Jumbo had already put to use, a tin of brightly coloured dye to dump into the water to attract the attention of any planes flying above, and a flare gun.

Jumbo was aware of his rough position when the Liberator ditched: twelve miles west northwest of Longships Lighthouse – a lighthouse just over a mile off the coast of Land's End in Cornwall. There was only one option, to row towards land.

The late November afternoon sunlight had disappeared and with the thick cloud cover there was little moonlight and no sign of the stars. The temperature was soon below zero and the only sound was that of the waves. Occasionally the engine drone of a high-altitude plane would be heard, but with the low cloud level the chance of being spotted was nigh on impossible. Nobody knew he was there. Jumbo continued to try and row using the limited capabilities of the aluminium oars.

The Atlantic Ocean at night was a far cry from the Long Beach Marine Stadium. However, that familiarity with a sporting life of long hours practising on the Thames gave Jumbo some succour. He knew he had to row almost twelve miles relying on kind currents, and the dread realisation was that he was now entering a heavily-mined area of the Atlantic.

Jumbo had to stay awake. His adrenaline levels were dropping and the acute pain of his injuries as well as the biting cold of the heavy sodden clothes were sapping what energy he had left. Hypothermia now became one further peril to face.

To survive, Jumbo would need to call upon an enormous amount of courage, determination and ability. He thought grimly back to 1926 and how his collapse in the Boat Race had been reported. These were the same personality traits that the Press had claimed that he conspicuously lacked.

The bright yellow life raft continued on its ponderous journey. Hours had passed and the oppressive darkness and cold continued to press down. In November, in that part of the seas, sunrise would not be until 07.30 hours. Jumbo's first task was to stay awake until sunrise, in the hope that visibility would have improved. He had to remain positive that daylight would reveal an outline of land on the horizon.

By 06.30 hours, he was too tired to row. The motion of the waves and the exhaustion were too much for him to stay awake. For an hour he drifted into and out of consciousness. At this hour, although he was unaware of his exact position, the life raft had travelled twenty-three nautical miles in a little over fourteen hours. Jumbo's efforts – and the fast-flowing ocean current – had guided his inflatable south-east. He had missed the safety of land.

With the sun beginning to rise, the inky blackness of the Atlantic was returning to a wintry white-flecked grey expanse.

At 07.30, HMT *Lincolnshire* – a converted fishing trawler – was continuing its patrol five miles off the Cornish mainland in a search for U-boats. A shout went up from the lookout who had spotted a bright yellow speck in the distance, rising and falling with the waves. The skipper, Lieutenant Samuel Larner, changed course and piloted his boat towards the yellow object.

At 07.45 Wing Commander Edwards was rescued. The crew of HMT *Lincolnshire* managed to carefully lift the badly injured, and unconscious, Olympian on board and Lieutenant Larner returned his vessel as quickly as he could to the harbour at Falmouth.

Mike, as well as Jumbo's mother and sister, were blissfully unaware of what had occurred until a telegram arrived from Jumbo to inform them that he had been in an incident but that he was safe, was recovering, and would see them soon.

On hearing the full story of the ditching, Mona, Jumbo's sister, wrote a letter of gratitude to Lieutenant Larner of HMT *Lincolnshire*.

56 Elsham Road, Kensington, W14, December 2nd 1943

Dear Lieutenant Larner

We have heard from my brother, Wing Commander Edwards, that he was lucky enough to be picked up by HMT Lincolnshire on the 22nd after his Liberator had been shot down off the Cornish coast. You and the crew were so good to him too and gave him dry clothes and grog, everything he needed on the way to Falmouth, and we want to say we've two brothers missing – one in Burma and one from RAF operations. 'Hugh' whom you rescued is the last one left.

If at any time you or any member of the *Lincolnshire* crew should want a room for a night in London, my mother and I have a spare room and would be very glad to put you up – everything is very simple as we have no help in the house, but rooms are very difficult to find sometimes in London, and we'd be glad if ours was even of use to you. The telephone is Park 4786, and is in the neighbourhood of Shepherd's Bush, Olympia and High Street Kensington. So please do not hesitate to invite yourself, any time, if we could be of use.

My brother is now off the danger list and is going on well, though he was very ill for some days after he came in – otherwise I expect he would have written to you himself.

With all our thanks for saving my brother from dying in his dinghy last month.

Your sincerely, *Mona Edwards*

A reply was forthcoming from Samuel Larner.

HMT Lincolnshire, GPO London

Dear Miss Edwards

I received your most grateful letter of December 2nd and I am glad to know your brother is off the danger list. The Officers and men of the *Lincolnshire* wish him a speedy recovery.

I am very glad to know that you appreciate what my Officers and men did for your brother. Of course I couldn't do a thing, my job was to get the ship in as soon as possible, so as to get medical assistance for I knew that your brother was seriously injured.

I wish to thank your mother and yourself most profoundly on behalf of myself and crew for the offer which you have given us. Once again we all wish your brother a speedy recovery.

I am yours truly, *S. Larner, Skipper, Lieutenant RNR*

For Jumbo, that was the end of his flying missions for the 53 Squadron and the RAF. With a stay in hospital, followed by four months back at home recuperating from his injuries, Jumbo had the time to write letters to the families of those lost in the Atlantic.

Prior to every mission, Jumbo would type out the names and addresses of the next of kin for all of his crew. His dread was that he would need to refer to the list, but it was now his duty to write and explain what had happened on the night of November 21st.

RAF protocols did not allow Jumbo to include all of the details. Jumbo was only permitted to write that the Liberator that he was piloting had been shot down by enemy fire and had ditched into the sea. He was able to convey the heroism that his crew had shown in the mission and throughout their career with 53 Squadron.

The hardest letter to write was that to Gisele Shield – the wife of his 23-year-old gunner, Warrant Officer George Shield. George had survived the initial ditching and had managed to clamber, badly injured, onto the broken fuselage of the Liberator. He was also the only one of Jumbo's crew that was a father. Jacqueline Francoise Shield was born on August 15th, 1943, just three months before her father died. George had been one of the crew that Jumbo had trained for 53 Squadron – over the past two months they had been together on over twenty training flights. One of these flights was to RAF Ballykelly in Northern Ireland, and George had just enough time to rush from the airfield and out to a local shop to buy a toy rabbit for his newborn daughter.

Jumbo kept the portraits of two of his lost crew in his logbook: Bruce Hamilton (middle) and Francis Halliday (bottom).

Wing Commander Hugh R. A. Edwards DFC, AFC. Reproduced with permission of the Imperial War Museum, London.

A few years later when Jacqueline was three years old, she told her mother that a nice man dressed in blue had come to her room in the night, sat on the bed and gently handed her the precious toy rabbit.

After the handwritten letters to the families had been sent out, Jumbo also typed out a report for his superiors with the heading 'The Last Flight of Liberator A/53'.

On March 29th, 1944, *The Times* reported that the King had approved the award of the Distinguished Flying Cross to Wing Commander Edwards, in recognition of gallantry and devotion of duty in the execution of air operations against the enemy. It did nothing to ease the feeling of guilt he had with the fortune of his survival and the tragic loss of his crew.

Chapter 18

Return to the Water

After weeks and months of recuperation, Jumbo returned to duty with 53 Squadron. The recuperation was physical, allowing his body time to recover from his life-threatening injuries. However, the mental scars were deep. He had lost his two brothers, he had lost his crew, and he had seen friends not return from missions. These were scars that would never fully heal.

In July 1944, Wing Commander Edwards DFC, AFC, was promoted – temporarily – to Group Captain. He was assigned to oversee operations at RAF Ballykelly, on the north coast of Northern Ireland, which provided a base for further Liberator patrols over the Atlantic. The days and nights of flying missions were now over for Jumbo but he was determined not to spend the rest of his days behind a desk in the squadron HQ. He insisted on returning to the cockpits of a variety of RAF training planes, such as the Miles Mentor and Airspeed AS.10 Oxford. Once more he was instructing the trainee pilots and navigators to be fully prepared for hostilities.

Jumbo was also back flying Liberators and training crews, with short flights over the Atlantic and performing depth charge bombing runs.

By the start of 1945, the U-boat threat had lessened due to the increased effectiveness of Coastal Command in detecting and destroying the enemy. The Germans were now being forced to operate out of bases in Norway and Germany. However, as the last year of the war dawned, the Germans regained some ground in the technology battle. Grand Admiral Dönitz had not yet given up hope of achieving strategic effect in the U-boat war and new faster types of U-boat were being constructed.

In an attempt to reimpose the fear of the U-boat, Admiral Dönitz ordered U-boat operations in British home waters. As a consequence, 53 Squadron was ordered to Reykjavik in Iceland. The Squadron were needed to help cover the sea area between Scotland and Iceland and to protect the convoys from these new German U-boats.

The climate that 53 Squadron encountered in the Icelandic winter was slightly different from that of Cornwall or Hampshire. It was immediately evident that the Liberators did not take well to the bitterly cold conditions and serious icing problems were encountered. For Group Captain Edwards and his men it was also a hostile environment to acclimatise to with snow banks and freezing conditions within the living and recreational quarters. Frequent snow blizzards would put the airstrip out of action for days.

On May 8th, 1945, the war in Europe ended. Germany unconditionally surrendered its military forces to the Allies, and the celebrations began. At Reykjavik, Jumbo ordered the beer to be distributed.

Squadron Leader Roy Stansfield was on a patrol in his Liberator when news filtered through to his crew that there had been an important announcement.

'I was flying an anti-U-boat control from our base in Iceland. We were escorting convoy UR 162, which was on its way from the UK. The sortie was uneventful, but radio messages told that something was up. On approaching base on return, about twenty to thirty miles away, we could see a big display of fireworks, signal cartridges etc. We realised that something had happened. We landed after twelve hours in the air and were met by a group of RAF not exactly sober (keen celebrations). We were debriefed, but couldn't celebrate ourselves because there was no beer left.'

Despite the ending of the war in Europe, the patrols of 53 Squadron continued until June 7th. These patrols were put in place to ensure rogue U-boat commanders had not ignored the surrender instructions, or if there was a need to help escort surrendering vessels to port. Several U-boats made their way to Reykjavik and Jumbo with his aircrews were able to visit the sort of ships that they had been chasing since 1941.

On July 31st, Jumbo took the controls of Liberator FK225. With a crew of four he took off from the barren airstrip at Reykjavik and flew back to Ballykelly and Northern Ireland. From there he journeyed back to Oxfordshire and a reunion with a relieved and celebratory family.

Six weeks later and the celebrations continued. On September 15th, three hundred pilots – dubbed 'the last of the few' – participated in a Battle of Britain display above London. This was the first major RAF fly-past of the post-war period and was part of the nationwide Thanksgiving Week events – commemorating the day in 1940 when the Luftwaffe lost sixty-one aircraft against the twenty-eight of the RAF. Millions of Londoners watched the display as it passed over the city and suburbs headed by Group Captain Douglas Bader flying a Spitfire.

In similar celebrations a thousand miles away, Jumbo was back in Reykjavik and in a Miles Martinet performing an aerobatic display to the thrill of the Icelandic crowds. At the end of Jumbo's display the first President of the newly established republic of Iceland, Sveinn Björnsson, asked the guests and spectators to hail Group Captain Edwards and the RAF with a four-fold 'hurrah'.

In the following months Jumbo continued the administration of 53 Squadron and oversaw the decommissioning of the Reykjavik airbase – the base was handed over to the Icelandic Government in 1946.

In August 1946, Jumbo was assigned to Coastal Command Headquarters. Coastal Command still maintained air-sea-rescue and reconnaissance duties but over the next few years there was a continued disbandment of combat units and the aircraft were transferred to the RAF Transport Command.

The Icelandic population were invited to 'Victory in Europe' celebrations at Reykjavik airbase, with Hugh performing an aerobatic demonstration, September 1945.

There was now more time with the family. Jumbo's sons, John and David, had spent their early years at various airfields throughout the Second World War, watching and waiting for their father to return for visits. When Mike and the boys were living in their cottage high on the Berkshire Downs, Jumbo would fly his plane low over the roof to let everyone know by the roar of engines that he was back safely and needed a lift home from the airfield.

In 1947, Jumbo was appointed as Station Commander of RAF Bassingbourn, Cambridgeshire, one of the main airfields for long-range transport aircraft. In 1948, Avro York, Avro Lancaster and Douglas Dakota aircraft from the base took part in the Berlin Airlift, a massive operation transporting essential commodities to the beleaguered city that would continue until the Autumn of 1949.

By 1948, it had been sixteen years since Jumbo had won his two gold Olympic gold medals and said his farewells to the sport of rowing. He had nothing left to prove. Nothing more to achieve. However, in 1948 rowing was integrated as a sport in the RAF – it demonstrated 'commitment to team before self, to sport and fitness and to having fun'.

Wing Commander Francis Hellyer had coached Cambridge to victory in the Boat Race of 1936. He was better known to his friends as 'Two-Legs' – he had lost both of his legs in an air crash in the First World War.

'Two-Legs', as Jumbo recalled, 'asked me if I would help coach the RAF crew for the Thames Challenge Cup at Henley. I laughed at the idea and told him I was completely out of touch and had forgotten all I knew about the art and technique of rowing.'

However, it did not take too much persuasion for Hellyer to recruit Jumbo to the cause. The appeal of taking a group of inexperienced RAF recruits and coaching them in an eight to compete at Henley Royal Regatta was too much of a challenge for Jumbo to resist.

They were entered in the Thames Challenge Cup, a competition for eights and aimed at club crews below The Ladies' Challenge Plate standard. The inexperienced RAF eight were not predicted to pose too much of a challenge for the twenty-nine other crews. They soon showed how well coached they were.

In the Heats the RAF defeated Trinity Hall, Cambridge, followed by Bedford Rowing Club. Weybridge Rowing Club were next to be surprised by the RAF eight, then Reading University were defeated in the semi-final. An experienced and strongly fancied Princeton University awaited them in the final. There was to be no fairytale victory for the RAF, the vastly more experienced American eight won by almost three lengths.

Understandably, Jumbo was incredibly proud of the RAF crew and what they had achieved together. 'After this I was asked by Two-Legs, who was head coach, if I would join his team to coach Oxford for the 1949 Boat Race. There is a difference between coaching a Thames Cup crew and a Varsity crew, and not least that of the weight of responsibility upon the coach. I protested that, although I was highly honoured to be asked, I simply did not feel competent to do so.'

Jumbo's absence from the river was seen as a distinct advantage. The Oxford coaches had witnessed what Jumbo had achieved with his RAF eight, and there was a belief that he could bring a freshness to Oxford that was so badly needed. 'So, when the President wrote to me I accepted the invitation to take over on the tideway as finishing coach.'

The coaching demands for a Varsity eight were high. With selection of a crew starting in October, and with the Boat Race usually scheduled for March, it was impractical to expect one man to undertake all the

John (left) and David (right) Edwards, photographed in 1945.

coaching. From some time around the 1860s, the Blue Boats were increasingly coached by a team of volunteer coaches, overseen by a nominated head coach.

During the selection of a crew, there are more rowers than a single coach can properly handle, so usually a number of past Blues were called in to help separate the wheat from the chaff. Along the way, the coach would become increasingly hands on until the time of the trail eights race, when an indicative selection would be made for the final eight.

The selection of the crew provided the opportunity for the coach to turn the eight over to a starting coach whose job would be to get the crew moving together, and to instil one single style throughout the boat. The crew would then be returned to the inscrutable gaze of the head coach in January.

From that point on, the head coach would generally take the crew for most of the time – occasionally with others taking a session or two. About two or three weeks out from the race, the head coach would bring in a finishing coach. It was the task of the finishing coach to sharpen the crew up and get them racing a couple of strokes a minute faster than they were before. The finishing coach would concentrate on starts and the transition to the stride, as well as the final sprint. This was the role that Jumbo had been recruited for.

To prepare, Jumbo re-read *A Textbook of Oarsmanship* by Gilbert Bourne and Steve Fairbairn's *Rowing Notes* – the two books which had been such an influence to Jumbo when he was developing the art of rowing.

Along with Hellyer as the coordinating coach, the coaching team consisted of another former Cambridge coach – James MacNabb – along with an Oxford Blue – Alexander McCulloch. As well as coaching Cambridge, MacNabb had won gold in the coxless four at the Olympic Games in 1924, and McCulloch had won silver in the single sculls in 1908. For Jumbo, watching James MacNabb row in 1924 alongside his famous 'Trinity four' was 'the nearest thing to perfection that I had seen, so I was not unhappy to try to coach for that.'

Cambridge had easily won the last two Boat Races – by ten lengths in 1947, and five lengths in 1948 – and it was hoped that this experienced coaching team, with Jumbo providing fresh ideas, would lead the Dark Blues to victory.

The 95th Boat Race in 1949 was heralded as a classic. Oxford took an early lead and were half a length ahead after the first minute of the race. By the time the crews passed the Mile Post, Oxford had extended their lead to a length. In the headwind along Chiswick Reach, and near the spot where Jumbo had his fateful collapse, Cambridge slowly redressed the balance. Cambridge drew level and the two crews passed under Barnes Bridge side-by-side. Despite numerous spurts from Oxford's stroke Davidge, Cambridge kept in touch and refused to allow Oxford to pull ahead.

Commentating for the BBC from a launch whose engine had failed, John Snagge announced to his millions of listeners the immortal line: 'I can't see who's in the lead, but it's either Oxford or Cambridge'.

Both crews were rating over thirty-three strokes per minute as they approached the finishing post. Cambridge, in one last momentous effort, just edged ahead to win by a quarter of a length.

The winning distance was the narrowest since the 'dead heat' result of the 1877 Race. The rowing correspondent for *The Manchester Guardian* declared that this was a race that 'will never be forgotten'. The correspondent for *The Times* claimed that '1949 must go down in Boat Race history as having provided one of the epic struggles of all time'.

Jumbo, along with his coaching team, was disappointed with the narrow loss but encouraged at the efforts put in by the crew. 'I think we were as fast as Cambridge and it was only their "winning tradition" that pulled them through, together with our greater expenditure of effort over the first half of the course.'

Another factor in Oxford's defeat was – according to Jumbo – their appearance. The Cambridge coach was Harold Rickett, who had travelled with Jumbo out to Los Angeles for the 1932 Olympics. Harold was in the eight that finished fourth in those Games, but he had gone on to coach Cambridge to victory in the Boat Race of 1948, and now a further victory a year later. Jumbo would sum up Harold as 'a great showman, and who never allowed his crew to be seen at a disadvantage. They were immaculately turned out, well disciplined and splendidly drilled, and in every way most impressive in their appearance. Oxford by comparison were the dead-end kids.'

Jumbo quickly rushed out to Foyles bookshop and acquired the book *Gamesmanship*, by Stephen Potter. In this humorous book – though one that Jumbo took quite seriously – the author illustrated how to secure an unfair advantage, purporting to show how poor players can beat better ones by subtle psychological ploys: the art of winning games without cheating. 'Harold was a past master of the College of Oneupmanship. I set myself the task of learning it but it was another eleven years before Oxford willingly accepted the necessary showmanship and discipline.'

Appearance and discipline would become two of the main foundations of Jumbo's coaching in the years to come.

Chapter 19

Dark Blue Redemption

The following year, 1950, 'Two-Legs' Hellyer and Alexander McCulloch stepped down from their Oxford coaching duties – but Jumbo and James MacNabb remained. *The Manchester Guardian's* rowing correspondent declared that Cambridge's crew was 'generally acknowledged to be one of the best seen on the tideway', and that 'Oxford could not, short of shipwreck or piracy, win the 1950 race'.

Oxford rowed valiantly in the Boat Race but Cambridge – coxed by Antony Armstrong-Jones (later to be the 1st Earl of Snowdon) – won by three and a half lengths. It was a fourth successive win for the dominant Light Blues.

In 1951, a decision was made by the President not to invite Jumbo to coach. 'I was not invited to coach, mainly because Christopher Davidge who was President, being tired of the run of defeats, decided to try a crew mainly composed of Etonians with Etonian coaches. Unhappily, it didn't work out.'

Oxford, battling against sizeable waves caused by a strong wind blowing against the tide, were struggling from the start. As Jumbo watched on from the confines of London Rowing Club, Oxford were taking on board a considerable amount of water. The Dark Blues shipped more water until they became entirely submerged, and had to be rescued by spectators on the Oxford launch *Niceia*.

Not since 1925 – and Sphinx with his Oxford crew – had there been a sinking in the Boat Race. The umpire quickly called a halt to the still rowing Cambridge and the race was declared a 'no row' – re-scheduled for two days later on Easter Monday. The re-row went only slightly better for the Dark Blues in that they stayed afloat. Cambridge won by a massive margin of twelve lengths, securing their fifth consecutive victory and another win for Harold Ricketts as coach. It was the largest winning margin for fifty-one years.

Having endured a humiliating defeat, Oxford president Adrian Stokes invited Jumbo back to join the coaching rotation for the 1952 Oxford boat. There was one problem though. Jumbo had been stationed to Bad Eilsen, twenty miles west of Hanover in West Germany.

Bad Eilsen hosted the headquarters of the RAF in the British Zone of Occupation and Group Captain Edwards was their new Senior Personnel Staff Officer. Jumbo took three weeks leave to coach the crew right before their race, but also felt it was his duty to meet the other coaches at regular intervals to discuss progress and selection. These coaching get-togethers took place over the winter months and Jumbo had been told that if these ventures back to England were to interfere in any way with his RAF duties, then he would not be allowed to coach.

Having secured the use of a twin-engine Avro Anson fighter plane, Jumbo would fly single-handedly during the rigours of a European winter from Germany to England and back – in one weekend. This required some detailed scheduling.

'The system I worked out enabled me to have breakfast in the mess on Saturday morning, and then to drive two miles to Bückeburg Airport, where I filed a flight plan with Air Traffic Control, picked up the Anson and took off at 10.00 hours (09.00 hours GMT). The launch left the OUBC at 13.25, so I had four hours for the flight, which took three and a half hours with a westerly wind and half an hour for a refuelling stop at Eindhoven. If there was no wind, I could do the trip in three hours non-stop. Mike was waiting at Abingdon at 13.00 hours with a car, so I had five minutes to clear customs and report to Air Traffic Control, ten minutes to drive over Boar's Hill to Folly Bridge and ten minutes to walk down the towpath and embark on the launch. On the return to Germany, I left Abingdon at 14.00 hours on Sunday, and went back non-stop, arriving about nightfall. Over two years I was never late in getting to Oxford or back to my Headquarters in Germany.'

The 98th Boat Race was scheduled for March 29th, but there were serious doubts that it could go ahead. A major snowstorm had descended on the country and a number of sporting events in London had already been cancelled for that Saturday.

The Cambridge crew – on a winning streak of five victories – were once again installed as favourites.

At stroke, Oxford had Peter Gladstone – the great-grandson of the 19th Century Liberal Prime Minister William Gladstone. Also in the crew was Christopher Davidge – the President for the previous year's humiliating defeat. Davidge came up to Oxford in 1948, and having stroked Eton to victory in the Ladies' Plate at Henley he already had a great reputation as a talented rower. He stroked Oxford in the thrillingly close Boat Race of 1949 and won the Stewards' at Henley in record time in the same year. Since then, Davidge had the bitter experience of an almost unbroken record of failure – culminating in the heavy loss the previous year.

Freddie Page, Oxford's coordinating coach, felt that however good Davidge might have been in the past, it would be a psychological error to allow him to stroke for this year's Boat Race. Not only had the crew no confidence in him, but Cambridge had his measure. However, after consulting with the coaches, Freddie made the decision to swap the positions of Gladstone and Davidge in the boat. Davidge was reinstated at stroke. With three weeks to go until the race, this change in the boat was seen by Jumbo as a measure of desperation – and was reported as so by the Press.

'It was in this atmosphere of despair that I took over the crew as fin-

The Oxford crew and Jumbo (third from the right) relax with a visit to Elstree Studios and a meeting with the American actor Van Heflin, 1952 © Teresa Stokes.

ishing coach on March 10th, with only three weeks to build the structure on the sound foundation laid by my fellow coaches. I drew up a balance sheet to see how we stood, and on the debit side I put down Cambridge's superiority of speed, the moral factors, the reputation of Harold Rickett (their unbeaten head coach), and their winning tradition. On the credit side, the only thing I could find to put down was the spirit of the Oxford crew.'

Nonetheless, as Jumbo was well aware, spirit was a fantastic quality to have and it gave hope.

With Christopher Davidge now reinstated at stroke, Jumbo needed to build up his confidence. 'I turned to him and said, "Christopher, a lot depends on you. The famous coach, Two-Legs Hellyer, used to say that although you were a good stroke now, you had it in you to become a classic stroke".'

The day before the race, Jumbo took his crew to Elstree Studios for a tour around the film studios. It was a means of getting their minds off the nerves that were building up.

A strong northerly wind was blowing, and the snowstorm that had been threatening over the past day or so finally arrived.

That evening, the Press were constantly ringing up the coaches to ask if the race would be postponed because of the blizzard. The reply that Jumbo gave was the same: the race would take place as arranged at 3.15 p.m. – it had never been postponed for a blizzard in more than one hundred and twenty years.

The following morning, the snowstorm was still raging, the wind still biting. Jumbo decided to forego the tradition of a morning practice but was delighted to learn that Cambridge had gone out and had returned frozen and miserable.

It was now an hour before the start, and Jumbo gathered his crew around him for his final talk.

Good coaches are usually associated as outstanding orators or high-powered salesmen; Jumbo was neither. He was by nature taciturn and a man of few words – and the experience of war had likely made him more so – but his few, carefully measured words before practice outings still managed to transform oarsmen into dedicated disciples of his cause. An Oxford Blue once said that if Edwards told the crew they would go faster by using teaspoons they would believe him.

Jumbo spoke quietly but with passion about his belief in them, that if they could keep close to Cambridge at the Mile Post the race would be theirs. Cambridge were on the defensive with nothing to gain and everything to lose.

Jumbo finished the speech with a resounding, 'You can win, and you **must** win'.

Adrian Stokes was asked to write a report on the race for the 1952 *Eagle Sports Annual*, a hugely popular comic aimed at boys. In the article, Stokes recollected the drama of that afternoon.

> 'It was still snowing hard when we came up to the stake-boats moored in the middle of the river. There was no time to think how

cold we were. Off came our sweaters, a man grabbed the rudder and held it level with that of the Cambridge boat, and then the Umpire stood up in his launch with his flag raised. He dropped it and we were off.

Ten strokes of blind fury and then the thought "This is it!"

The boat was bumping in the rough water, and there was the enemy alongside. Perhaps a little ahead? Never mind Cambridge, think of putting every ounce of energy into driving the boat through the waves!

After a couple of minutes we got our second wind and it was easier to think clearly.

I could hear the roar of the crowd and the shouts of the coxes. Harrods' great building loomed through the mist, and Cambridge were still alongside. They had failed to get their lead, and now the bend was in our favour; they must have been rattled out of their stride.

Through the deafening noise of the crowd on Hammersmith Bridge, I somehow found the breath to yell: "Lovely stuff, boys."

Just after Hammersmith we saw the Light Blue blades almost touching ours and the coxes were shouting at each other. Nobody touched and we plugged on, our hands numb with the bitter cold and beginning to feel the strain in our legs and shoulders. "We ought to get away here," we thought, with the long bend to go round and smoother water; but Cambridge hung on. We tried to shake them off with sudden spurts, but they would not give in.

Now we had had the last of our bend, but Christopher Davidge was driving us along quite unperturbed. There is one thing about a close race… it keeps you from thinking how tired and agonizingly uncomfortable you feel. The bend came round in Cambridge's favour. We were aching all over, but we knew we could still do it; they must have been feeling worse.

We shot Barnes Bridge almost level, and the coxes had another argument. I was now only conscious of the rhythm of the boat and the Light Blue blades so near ours.

A visibly cold Christopher Davidge, with Jumbo alongside, shortly after winnning for Oxford the 'finest Boat Race of the Century', 1952
© *Illustrated London News Group.*

This was the worst moment. We were on the outside of the last bend, and doubt assailed me. I did not see how on earth I could row another stroke or draw another breath; but then I saw out of the corner of my eye that the Light Blue blades were splashing badly. All doubt was gone, my aching limbs forgotten. I shouted with what felt like all the breath I had: "We can do it!"

Stroke's blade bit harder into the water, and the whole crew seemed to come to life. "They" were beaten, rowed out, with two minutes to go. They were the longest two minutes of my life, but I did not mind so long as Cambridge were slipping astern.

The grim Mortlake Brewery was in sight. Where was that winning-post? Our gallant enemy were ten feet behind, then one more stroke, and up went the Dark Blue flag. Gasping for breath and pouring with sweat, we were the nine happiest men in England!

Davidge was the hero of the day. He had stroked brilliantly and avenged his narrow defeat of 1949. But he could not have done it by himself. Every man in the crew backed him up all the way, and the cox had steered magnificently in the blinding snow and mist.'

Oxford had won by a 'canvas' – approximately nine feet. The narrowest margin of victory since 1877. At no point during the course of the race did either boat have a clear water advantage over their opponent.

Jumbo had his first victory at the Boat Race, as either a rower or a coach. More importantly to him, Oxford had ended their dismal run of five consecutive defeats.

Not since Jumbo had proved his critics wrong at Henley in 1931 had he felt prouder.

Chapter 20
The Four Pillars

The 'Boat Race of the Century' had given back to Oxford a sense of pride. The memorable victory had persuaded Jumbo to remain on the coaching team, determined to create a new Oxford – one that was forged in his belief of four main tenets. These four pillars that created the framework for 'speed and success' were fitmanship, oarsmanship, crewmanship and morale. It was imperative to Jumbo that a crew worked together to achieve all four.

In Jumbo's book on coaching techniques, *The Way of a Man with a Blade*, he succinctly summarised each virtue.

Fitmanship consisted of physique, strength, stamina and the way to achieve it.

Oarsmanship was the art of using the most powerful muscles to the best advantage.

Crewmanship was the practical application of that art – including the boat itself, the rig and the oars.

Morale encapsulated experience, determination, confidence and past success.

One lesson that Jumbo learnt at an early age – when he put his complete trust into the machinery that was lifting him into the skies for air races – was the need to plan meticulously. 'When you realise what is wrong, half your troubles are over. The next step is to plan how to put them right.'

Being prepared had saved Jumbo's life on many occasions – most notably when battling against the Germans over Europe and the Atlantic. A plan 'needs thought, courage and action now. It is simply not good enough just to hope for the best, or to trust that things will turn out right in the end'.

However, Jumbo's continuing role with the RAF – and being based in West Germany – meant that he could only contribute as a finishing coach, and not take on the role of head coach.

In 1953, Jumbo continued his weekend commutes to England in his borrowed Anson. The 99th Boat Race was held on March 28th and thankfully for all concerned the weather was more Spring-like than the blinding blizzard of the previous year.

In the build-up to the race, opinions were once more divided on which crew was favourite to win. According to the rowing correspondent of *The Manchester Guardian*, upon arrival at Putney Oxford demonstrated 'great superiority' over Cambridge – yet the Light Blues had improved, and had 'the pace, if not the form, to win'.

The race was not the classic of the previous year, and Cambridge won with ease by a resounding eight lengths. Cambridge were dominant once more, avenging their defeat.

By 1954, Jumbo had finished his role as Senior Personnel Staff Officer in West Germany. He was now back in England, stationed at Coastal Command Headquarters in North London. This was to be his last posting.

That year, 1954, had an extra special meaning for both Jumbo and the British public – it was the 100th Boat Race.

The preparations for Oxford were disrupted a few weeks prior to the race day. The crew had been struck down by influenza in training and had to reshuffle their order.

During the build-up to the 100th Boat Race, the rowing correspondent for *The Times* had suggested that 'until three weeks ago a Cambridge victory seemed almost certain' but practice rows had proved disappointing. Although the new order of Oxford 'seemed weak', they made better progress in training than Cambridge. Yet the Light Blues, who were described as 'well drilled' nevertheless remained 'precarious favourites.'

On April 3rd, the two crews lined up at the starter mark for the 100th Boat Race. Oxford made the better start, but at the Mile Post both crews were alongside one another.

The turning point of the race came at Chiswick Reach and with the wind now nearly dead ahead the water became increasingly choppy. Cambridge were suffering from the rough water in the middle of the river and – by Barnes Bridge – Oxford were a good three lengths in front. Oxford drew further away and victory was theirs – by four and a half lengths. The Dark Blues had now won two of the last three Boat Races – and integral to this success was the coaching of Jumbo.

The following two years were not successful. 'We lost in 1955 and 1956. Although at least one of these crews was fast, the standard of oarsmanship was really of a very low order, but as finishing coach I could do nothing about improving it.'

After twenty-five eventful years, Group Captain Edwards DFC, AFC, retired from the RAF and Coastal Command in 1956. Jumbo could now dedicate more of his time to Mike – to whom he would write constantly from Germany to implore her to not keep spending their money – and to coaching the crew.

In 1957, the Oxford President was Rod Carnegie – a revolutionary Australian who invited Jumbo to coach for six weeks in the middle of training. Carnegie had given a lot of thought to the causes of the previous two defeats and was determined to win the Boat Race, even if it meant breaking from the traditional way of doing things.

Concerned about Carnegie's revolutionary methods, Jumbo declined the invitation to coach but in the end was persuaded to help. When Carnegie insisted on using 'American rig' it was too much for one of the coaches, Antony Rowe, to stomach, and he resigned. Jumbo ploughed on, regarding it his duty in the middle of training to 'teach the crew how to row'.

Jumbo was pained to find the crew lacking in oarsmanship. 'When there was so much to be done in teaching basic oarsmanship, neither the training punt, *Leviathan*, nor a tub pair was made available to me. So, I resigned.'

Having resigned his position as coach, Jumbo feared that all his previous hard work to improve the standards of Oxford would dissipate. Already developing a reputation for imperiousness, Jumbo lost a lot of support and credibility by this action.

'I now forfeited the respect and sympathy of Oxford's supporters by resigning and leaving Oxford in the lurch. I was, for the time being, an outcast again.'

Despite this chaotic situation with the resignations of Jumbo and Antony Rowe, the Oxford crew were fast and heavily favoured by the Press onlookers. The rowing correspondent of *The Times* summarised the form of the crews, 'Never in the past ten years has there been such unanimity in Boat Race forecasts as this year, when only the staunchest Cambridge supporters could see more than an outside chance of a Light Blue victory'. Oxford lost by two lengths.

For Jumbo, watching on from the bank, Oxford's physical strength in the boat should have resulted in a win by five lengths. 'Something fundamental went wrong, and they were beaten. They were grossly over-confident and decided to row the race without any regard for Cambridge. This doesn't work in the Boat Race.'

Cambridge had now won the last three Boat Races, and Jumbo could only look on in frustration.

Chapter 21

Mutiny on the Isis

Jumbo's two sons, John and David, had inherited their father's love of the river. As students at Downside School in rural Somerset, John had helped to found the Downside Rowing Club and David joined his brother in the boat.

In 1953, John followed in his father's footsteps and went up to Christ Church, Oxford. Two years later, his younger brother David joined him. As with Jumbo and Sphinx before them, the Edwards brothers rowed together in several Christ Church crews over the next few years and won the Oxford University Boat Club fours in 1956. That same year the brothers also rowed in a pair together and won the inaugural Amateur Rowing Association National Championships in 1956. They had inherited their father's talent.

In 1958, Jumbo was invited back into the Oxford coaching fold. His fear of being an outcast after he had resigned from his coaching duties was unfounded. Oxford needed him once more.

Selected at stroke was 20-year-old Christ Church undergraduate David Edwards. Jumbo had coached his sons before, both at Downside and at Christ Church, and so David was not unfamiliar with the idiosyncrasies of his father's methods.

David Edwards, the youngest son of Jumbo, and selected at stroke for Oxford, 1958.

For Cambridge, the legendary Harold Rickett had also made a return to coaching duties. The last time Jumbo and Harold had gone up against one another was in 1952 when Oxford had triumphed. Rowing at number six for the Light Blues was Peter Rickett, Harold's son. This would be the first time in the history of the Boat Race in which each crew included the son of one of its coaches.

The Press were not entirely convinced that this would be Oxford's year. Three weeks before the big day, Oxford had taken delivery of a new boat. The boat, built by George Sims of Hammersmith, was designed on distinctly American lines, with a pronounced sheer fore and aft. This earned the Oxford boat the nickname of the 'banana boat'. The outriggers, too, were of a new pattern – designed by Jumbo in his quest to perfect the fastest boat.

The Times reported on the progress of the crew a few weeks before the race: 'Clearly Oxford have better rhythm and more steadiness with D. Edwards in the boat. But though it would be unfair to offer much criticism of their first outing in a new boat, it was apparent that neither their paddling nor their rowing was effective.'

At number six, Oxford did possess a talented and effective American rower – Yale oarsman Reed Rubin who had lobbied the coaches to switch to the American-designed boat. It was noted by *The Times* that 'No American since the war has been in the losing crew'. This was perhaps an ill-fated omen.

The 104th Boat Race was a battle of the legendary coaches – Jumbo and Harold – and their sons.

The course was shrouded in a London fog but the crowd on the banks could just make out that Cambridge had started strongly. By the Mile Post, Cambridge led by a length. Edwards at stroke responded, bringing the rate up to thirty-four, but the Oxford crew could make no impression. Able to relax, Cambridge passed the finishing post three and a half lengths clear of Oxford in the third fastest winning time in the event's history.

The Weekly Dispatch conjured up a vivid image for its readers, 'Group Captain H. R. A. Edwards, Oxford's coach, lit a cigarette on the umpire's launch with something of the panache of a man going out to face the firing squad, but he too could derive consolation from the fact that no one could have put up a braver fight than his own son at stroke'.

A week later, a letter arrived for Jumbo.

> 'Let me say frankly that I and others like-minded are **very** satisfied that Oxford was so thoroughly trounced in the Boat Race, in an **American** type canoe by **American** type rowing. Why oh why copy **America** in performing the time-honoured **British** event? If the misfortune of an Oxford win had been effected, it would have been a two-fold triumph for America to brag about. Let us rather uphold our own country, our style, our boat craft. Please, oh please, return loyally to our own country rather than make the futile attempt to copy America.
>
> Yours with the best intentions,
>
> *(Miss) M. A. Pett*
>
> (Please do not trouble to reply; I only put my name to prevent the odium of anonymity.)

Jumbo kept the letter. It is not known if he replied.

In the Summer of 1958, the disappointment of losing the Boat Race was quickly forgotten. In 1930, Jumbo had travelled to Canada and participated in the very first British Empire Games. Rowing for England, as Wales had opted not to submit a crew for the regatta, Jumbo returned home with two gold medals in the coxless fours and eights. In July 1958, Wales were hosting the British Empire and Commonwealth Games and Jumbo was proud to assist with the coaching of the Welsh rowing crews. The pride was even more so as his sons, David and John, were both selected for the coxless fours.

The 6th British Empire and Commonwealth Games featured just nine sports and all but the rowing were held in and around Cardiff. In the absence of a suitable location in South Wales for the rowing events, Llyn Padarn (Lake Padarn) was selected to host the regatta.

The lake, two miles long and overshadowed by the looming Mount Snowdon, could be serene one day and tempestuous the next. The weather laid down an early marker when five buoys marking out the rowing course were sunk by gale-force winds. This was in early July.

The regatta was beset by strong winds, whistling down from the mountains, and on the day of the finals the conditions were challenging. The Duke of Edinburgh had flown in to be present for the regatta, and to the crowd's delight they witnessed the coxless four of David Edwards, John Fage, David Prichard and John Edwards battle hard for a bronze medal – a fitting tribute to the Welsh heritage of the Edwards family.

From his vantage point in the Royal Enclosure, the Duke was also one of the first to notice that a judge's pontoon was beginning to sink rapidly into the lake.

Sadly, Jumbo's mother – Anne – had not returned to her Welsh homeland to witness her two grandsons win their bronze medal. Three days prior to her eighty-seventh birthday, Anne Edwards died at her home in London.

Anne had experienced the heartbreaking loss of four of her sons, but always followed with pride the rowing successes of Jumbo and her grandsons. She was laid to rest alongside her husband and two sons in the graveyard at Westcote Barton. A further memorial stone paid tribute to her two other sons, Sphinx and Oswald, who had been laid to rest in foreign soil.

Up to 1959, Oxford – as with Cambridge – would employ a team of rotating guest coaches. With Oxford, this was usually a team of four, and for Cambridge five: one of whom would be the head coach. At the beginning of the Oxford summer term, a new President – who was usually the most suitable Blue who had rowed in the previous Boat Race – was elected by a dozen Blues in residence and the Oxford college captains. The President would then send out an invite to a suitable candidate to take the main responsibility of coaching. In those days, there were no permanent appointments, and all the coaches were amateurs. None of them received payment; just a vote of thanks.

In the Summer of 1958, Ronnie Howard stood for President and won by a single vote against the Yale oarsman Reed Rubin. This narrowest of wins was the catalyst of what would be a tumultuous few months for Oxford.

The first controversial decision taken by Howard was to break with tradition and invite only one coach to take the training. Ronnie argued that there was only one man capable of delivering a victory in 1959: Jumbo.

The Times was dubious, 'It will be an interesting experiment, for the simple reason that few can give long periods of time to the task. It is sometimes said that twelve to thirteen weeks is too long for one man to hold the interest of the crew, but it is, of course, done regularly and successfully elsewhere by professional coaches.'

Jumbo as sole coach commenced the training of his crew. He remained true to the tenets of his 'art of rowing': fitmanship, oarsmanship, crewmanship and morale.

By the first week of October, rumours were rife amongst the rowing community that all was not well in the Oxford camp. Reed Rubin, who was selected for the crew despite the loss in 1958, and who had so narrowly missed out on the Presidency, was adamant that further coaches were required. Rubin was supportive of employing his former coach at Yale, Jim Rathschmidt. He was of the belief that his fellow American could guarantee an Oxford victory. This coaching, according to Howard in a disparaging response, would be achieved 'over the telephone'. Rubin's main complaint, however, was with Jumbo's training regime.

This rumble of disharmony soon became a cacophony. It made headlines in the newspapers.

On October 9th, *The Times* reported on the doubts that Rubin was experiencing:

> 'Rubin said today that he may not row next year. The President would have to convince him it would be worthwhile. He had no wish to criticise the President... "but it seems to me," said Rubin, "that if I am not in complete harmony with what is going on, it would be better if I was not in the crew." Rowing, he said, was a very delicate business, and harmony on the bank was just as important as harmony in the boat. In his three years in the Yale crew, he said, he covered as many miles as he did in one year with the Boat Race crew. He did not think it was a good thing to row more than two hours a day in training. It wasn't necessary to do more.'

On October 18th, the *Daily Mail* ran with the headline: 'Now it's MUTINY on the ISIS – Old Blues may form Pirate Boat Race Crew' – 'Six of the Oxford crew who lost the last Boat Race have threatened not to row in next year's race because they object to the present training methods.'

Jumbo was unique amongst rowing coaches to concentrate so much on fitness – or 'fitmanship' as he described it. He had blamed his own lack of fitness for his collapse in the Boat Race of 1926. Jumbo knew all about the level of opprobrium that would be directed to any of his crew who struggled physically, and his intense course of physical training was intended to prevent this.

He drew inspiration from the Austrian running coach Franz Stampfl. The strict regime involved interval training, techniques that had assisted

Roger Bannister to his famous breaking of the four-minute mile barrier.

On this fundamental, Jumbo was a coach ahead of his time.

Amongst the mutineers was Rubin's fellow American – Charles Grimes – who two years previously had won an Olympic gold medal in the American eight. Also amongst the mutineers, according to the newspapers, was Jumbo's youngest son: David Edwards.

David, who had stroked the Oxford boat in the 1958 defeat, had been moved to number six in the 1959 boat. Caught amongst the tumult, it was David's aim to maintain harmony in the crew as he saw this as the only way that they could win. He now had the unenviable task of walking the proverbial tightrope – balancing between ensuring that the crew and his close friends remained united and that his father remained as the head coach.

With the Press reporting on his son's decision to apparently side with the rebels, Jumbo angrily confronted David after a morning's training session. David's father accused him, unfairly, of betrayal.

The whole situation had become toxic.

As Peter Mallory summarised in *The Sport of Rowing*, the machinations of the rebellion went on for months. There were meetings both public and private, meetings held, meetings refused.

Finally in mid-October, according to rowing historian Chris Dodd, mutineers Charlie Grimes and Jonathan Hall – the OUBC Secretary – went to see Howard privately. 'They suggested that if Ronnie dropped Jumbo and accepted three Yale coaches whom they named, they would cooperate. The coaches they proposed were all from the 1956 Yale crew who had won the Olympic gold medal, the crew with whom Grimes had rowed'. Howard remained firm, he would stand by Jumbo.

Despite rather enjoying the public spat that their rivals were embroiled in, Mike Maltby, the President of Cambridge University Boat Club (CUBC), came out in support of Ronnie and Jumbo. 'I shall refuse to row against any Oxford crew who have not the support of their president.'

David Christie, Secretary of CUBC, wrote in the university newspaper:

> 'The group led by Reed Rubin are mostly losing Blues and none of them has any great rowing reputation. This action in itself shows a remarkable lack of responsibility and loyalty.'

Ronnie Howard's loyalty to Jumbo coupled with Cambridge insistence that they were only going to race against President Howard's crew resulted in the collapse of the mutiny in the first week of November.

Some sort of compromise was arrived at whereby most of the mutineers made themselves available under the coaching of Jumbo. Reed Rubin withdrew from the crew, citing his need to catch up on his academic studies. Rubin's fellow American, Charlie Grimes, was selected as was Jumbo's son, David. However, Grimes would often wear his trademark railroad engineer's hat and this was not apparel that Jumbo approved of.

Ever since 1949 and Jumbo's encounter with Harold Rickett's immaculately turned out Cambridge crew, he was determined that his crew would always present themselves in smart dress.

'The turn-out of a crew is important. A boat race crew is always on parade. What a difference it makes to the look of such a crew if at all times the cox is properly dressed in white trousers, blue blazer and cap. In 1958, on the first day on the tideway, one member of the Oxford crew elected to wear an old grey sweater, instead of the uniform blue. A crew in which such a lapse can occur is not a good crew, and needless to say we were beaten.'

So, when Jumbo demanded that Grimes remove his hat this caused a further issue with the American. This was the late 1950s and Jumbo's insistence on 'proper dress' was a hearkening back to the values that had stood him in good stead in his youth. A regularly heard mantra of Jumbo's was, 'if you are going to row for Oxford, then you have got to look like Oxford'. Charlie Grimes promptly walked out of the boathouse and left the crew.

In a profile on Jumbo published in *World Sport* shortly after Grimes departure, the article opens with 'Group Captain H. R. A. "Jumbo" Edwards – loved, hated, but never ignored'.

Jumbo's son, David, was also not immune from the fashion decrees of his father. 'How can you expect to go fast in the boat if your hair is not cut?', was the exasperated shout that David would have to endure if he had not visited the barber's and his hair had crept dangerously towards his shoulders. As David reminisced, 'My father always complained because I didn't like wearing socks in the boat and because he thought my hair was too long. When I was looking at some photos recently, I came across the picture of the 1932 Olympic four and Jumbo is in his Oxford Boat Race sweater without any socks on!'

With all of the intrigue surrounding the 'Crisis on the Isis', there was an even greater anticipation than usual for the 105th edition of the Boat Race. The quashing of the rebellion had created a unity in the Oxford boat. Jumbo still worked the crew hard on their fitness with constant circuit training, but he was also relying on the fourth of his pillars: morale.

After the rigours of the intense training sessions, Jumbo would settle the crew down and regale them with heroic anecdotes of battling against the odds. He would talk to his crew about the Athenians of 447BC who rowed two hundred miles from Piraeus to prevent a massacre; of the bravery of the slaves made to row the Roman triremes into battle; of how Sherlock Holmes used the rowing action of a perfect finishing stroke when he pitched Professor Moriarty off the ledge at the Reichenbach Falls; and of his uncle, Tommy Pryce VC, as he fought fearlessly against the overwhelming German forces.

Jumbo, though, would never talk about his own bravery over Essen as he faced the exploding flak, or of the superhuman strength he needed to row himself overnight in the Atlantic.

He would never speak about his war experiences to his family. There was too much death, too much loss, too much guilt for Jumbo to ever revisit those times when morale and a fighting spirit was all that kept him alive. Alcohol helped him forget – as so many of his fellow wartime veterans also discovered.

By March 1959, the Dark Blue crew were at a peak of fitness. The Press were undecided as to which of the crews were the favourites for a win. The Light Blues had won the previous four, but Oxford were displaying immense strength and posting quick times in the final week of practices.

The Birmingham Daily Post concluded that, 'The only certainty about this year's Boat Race is that Oxford are a better crew than last year, and Cambridge probably not quite so good'. The newspaper was also surmising that Oxford were a far better crew with having employed just the one coach. 'They have acquired a cohesion which Cambridge lacks'.

On Saturday, March 28th, the huge crowds flocked down to the Thames to watch the two crews battle it out. Reed Rubin was amongst the supporters, cheering on the Dark Blues from one of the boats following the crews down the course.

Oxford made a strong start and by the Mile Post were four seconds in front, and soon were a full length ahead of their rivals. By Hammersmith Bridge the Oxford crew had doubled their lead and were looking magnificent – rowing with consummate ease and power. Oxford continued to lengthen their lead, with Jumbo watching on from the following launch. David, rowing at six, heard the roar of the crowd as they shot under Barnes Bridge.

Oxford won by six lengths. It was Oxford's largest margin of victory in forty-seven years, and David had succeeded where his father and his Uncle Sphinx had failed – he had rowed in a winning Oxford boat.

The Times concluded their race report with, '...this year's Boat Race was a personal triumph for Group Captain Edwards, who successfully shouldered this tremendous responsibility [of being the only coach] and methodically built up a fine crew'.

Jumbo Edwards was now part of Boat Race folklore. In the Press, he was referred to as Oxford's 'legendary coach'.

Chapter 22

We Meet Again, Herr Krupp

With Jumbo as Head Coach, the redemptive victory of 1959 was followed by a further Oxford win the following year. This was the first time that Oxford had won consecutive Boat Races since the First World War. Jumbo, through his coaching methodology, had transformed the fortunes of Oxford. Most importantly he had established a winning mentality.

1960 was an Olympic year, and the rowing world was gathering at Lago di Albano – a picturesque lake sixteen miles south-east of Rome – for the regatta. After Jumbo's transformation of Oxford's fortunes, he was the outstanding candidate to coach the Great Britain eight for the Olympics. His crew would be the same eight that had won Oxford that year's Boat Race.

Hopes in the Press were high for the 1960 Olympic regatta.

> 'The British rowing team, widely regarded as the strongest ever sent from these islands to compete in an Olympic regatta, has made an impressive showing since practice started on Lake Albano. The form of the British eight, coached by Group Captain Hugh 'Jumbo' Edwards, has made a deep impression. This is not surprising, for the crew are probably, of all entries for the eights event, the most polished in technique'. (*The Times, August 29th, 1960*)

The crew may have been the most technically polished, but the success that was expected did not happen. The Great Britain eight came third in their heat – beaten by West Germany, the European champions – and, more surprisingly, by the French.

The repechage gave Great Britain one last chance to go through to the final. They were drawn to face the Americans and the Swedes. The eight rowed superbly in windy conditions but narrowly lost out to the Americans, by just over a second.

The British rowing team failed to win a single medal at the Olympics in Rome. Only the coxless four made it through to a final. The last time a Great Britain eight had won Olympic gold was in 1912. The failure in Rome was further proof that other countries had ousted Great Britain from her former position of rowing supremacy.

Other rowing nations had perfected the art of boat design, and Jumbo bemoaned the heaviness of the British boats.

'In Rome our boats seemed very old-fashioned and heavy. Our eight, one of the lightest and best ever built at Hammersmith was the biggest and heaviest boat there, weighing 299 lbs as compared with the 276 lbs of the Italians. It is fair to say that the winners could not have achieved their speeds using our boats'.

Ever since Jumbo started tinkering with the aerodynamics of his aeroplanes to ensure that they swept through the skies as quickly as possible, he was fascinated with improvements to equipment that would give an added advantage.

Now that he had integrated into Oxford a winning mentality and a strict training regime, he dedicated himself through the late 1950s and 60s to 'technical advancement'. He would spend his evenings in the development of long oars and 'spade' blades: Jumbo was among the first to appreciate that increasing boat speeds called for more severe gearing. He also introduced the use of ergometers to measure and develop physical strength, and strain gauges, accelerometers, and trace recorders to calculate work output throughout the stroke cycle.

We Meet Again, Herr Krupp

In his book *The Way of a Man with a Blade*, published in 1963, Jumbo set out his theories and experimentations. The book was also a cry from the heart of one who had watched British rowing accept its decline without a struggle.

Many of his technological inventions were met with scepticism.

'Immediately after the Boat Race of 1960 I set to work to build a gadget to operate a stop-watch that would assist the cox with calculating stroke rates. We asked Lucas, the instrument maker, to tidy it up, and they produced the transitional pulse rate counter. This remarkable meter excited tremendous interest at the Olympic Games in Rome, though at home it was the object of only mild interest or derision by the Press'.

Jumbo's experimentation with the dimension and shape of oar blades was also a constant. His expertise of aeronautics from his flying days was utilised in how to best streamline an oar. Jumbo made the connection of how the rowing blade acts 'like the wing of an aeroplane or a hydrofoil'. The oar blade was once believed to rip through the water, generating a drag force acting normal to the blade. Jumbo discovered that the oar blade acts as an aerofoil making use of lift forces to propel the boat through the water early and late in the stroke, with drag being the dominant propulsive force when the oar is perpendicular to the boat.

This tinkering was also an inspiration to Cambridge – in a rather different way. A rumour that the Light Blues had made a sensational modification to their oars was deliberately passed by informants to the Oxford headquarters. Within minutes, Jumbo was hurrying to investigate.

Leaning against the Cambridge boathouse he found an ordinary-looking oar, except that the blade had a serrated edge and a large hole in the centre. The story is told that Jumbo stood rubbing his chin, a little amazed, and then began taking measurements. When the boatsman arrived, Jumbo inquired: 'What on earth are the advantages?'. He was told, 'The serrated edge enables the blade to pass through the small waves more easily and helps for a clean finish of the stroke.' It wasn't until some hours later that the perplexed Jumbo was told that it was all a big hoax.

Princess Margaret is introduced to Jumbo and his Oxford crew, 1960.

In addition to the honour of coaching the Olympic eight, Jumbo was also invited to coach the most historic, prestigious and successful rowing club in the world: Leander Club. As a rower, Jumbo would ridicule the 'pink hat' brigade that made up the Leander membership and crews, but it was not a role that he was going to refuse. He would coach Leander at Henley Regatta, and at international regattas.

In 1961, Oxford had the chance to make it a hat-trick of successive wins in the Boat Race. Cambridge had not lost three consecutive races since 1913. The Dark Blues included five of the Great Britain crew who had narrowly lost out to the American eight in the Olympic repechage the previous year and were firm favourites.

Oxford won the toss and elected to start from the Surrey station, and soon established an early lead. By the Mile Post, and with the advantage of the bend in the river, Cambridge drew level. Oxford swept under Hammersmith Bridge a good length and a half ahead and held a clear water advantage. The geography of the river would now be to the advantage of the Dark Blues. Not only were they on the inside berth round the great left-hand bend into Chiswick Reach but Oxford's cox – P. J. Reynolds –

skilfully seized every possible advantage at a critical and difficult part of the course. Jumbo, following in the launch – and wearing his distinctive dark blue Oxford cap and sheepskin jacket – yelled out encouragement to the crew.

Reynolds called out for another spurt. It did not happen. This was the first indication to Jumbo that all was not well with the crew. Approaching Chiswick steps, the spectators on the bank, and the millions watching on television, could see that the Cambridge boat was rapidly closing the gap to their rivals. G. V. Cooper, rowing at six in the Oxford boat, had slumped over his oar. At the same point on the river that Jumbo had collapsed thirty-five years ago, the same fate had afflicted Cooper.

Cooper managed to recover but once again lurched sideways and sent the spray flying from his moving but ineffectual blade. Cambridge swept past the Oxford boat and won by a comfortable margin of four and a half lengths.

Cooper – who had rowed under Jumbo in the Olympic eight – was shattered. Jumbo tried to deflect any blame that the newspapers placed on Cooper by accepting the criticism for his design of the oars. For that year's Boat Race, Jumbo had again tinkered with the length of the oars – they were an unprecedented thirteen feet in length. One eminent expert wrote: 'Is the Boat Race the proper forum to try out major experiments in rig?'

Jumbo immediately declared that, 'We are reverting to the same rig as 1959, when we beat Cambridge by six lengths.' The sports journalist Harry Carpenter, writing for the *Daily Mail*, directly asked if it was Cooper's collapse that had influenced his decision. 'Obviously it had everything to do with it', retorted Jumbo. 'After what happened to Cooper there is no question of our using the same oars again'.

It was a rare admission by Jumbo that his constant experimentation with oar design had gone badly wrong – but it was also an attempt to protect Cooper from taking the blame. He also ensured that Cooper remained involved in Oxford rowing by inviting him as coach for Isis, the Oxford reserve crew.

Jumbo Edwards, Hügel Regatta, Essen, 1962.

Later that year, Jumbo took his Leander crew to the Hügel Regatta, one of the oldest and most prestigious international rowing regattas.

The Internationale Hügel Regatta takes place in Essen, Germany, and is named after the Villa Hügel which was built in the 19th Century by the industrialist Alfred Krupp as a residential home for his family.

Eighteen years previously, Jumbo had skilfully piloted his Hampden bomber through the barrage of exploding flak to a few hundred feet about the Krupp's steelworks and dropped his payload of incendiary bombs. He narrowly escaped with his life and that of his air crew.

This time, Jumbo and his crew were on a commercial airline and – in a far less eventful flight than the hair-raising one in 1943 – landed without incident at Cologne Bonn airport.

On arrival they were met by their German hosts. Jumbo and his fellow coach, Peter Sutherland, were led outside the airport and towards a waiting, and rather splendid, Mercedes car to meet the organiser of the regatta.

They were greeted by a distinguished looking man in his mid-fifties. He warmly shook the hand of Jumbo and introduced himself as Herr Alfried Krupp. Jumbo hid his surprise well. Alfried Krupp, the grandson of Alfred Krupp who had built up the Krupp industrial empire, became *de facto* head of the firm in 1941. Under Alfried, the company used slave labour supplied by the German government and often assigned Jewish prisoners from concentration camps to work in many of its factories.

After the war he was convicted of crimes against humanity and sentenced to twelve years imprisonment – of which he served three.

Jumbo sat in silence in the back of Alfried's Mercedes as they were driven through the streets of Cologne, back towards the city that he had bombed and that had tried to shoot him out of the skies.

On the way there, Herr Krupp turned to Jumbo and enquired, 'Ah, Group Captain, have you been to Essen before?' The laconic reply came – according to Peter Sutherland – in Jumbo's rather measured way: 'Yes, Herr Krupp, but I wasn't able to stay'.

A year later, in 1962, Edwards was appointed coach for the Welsh Commonwealth Games rowing team and he and his sons, David and John, headed out to Perth, Australia. The Welsh coxless four went one better than in 1958, winning silver, and narrowly missed out on gold by one second to England.

Throughout the 1960s, Jumbo continued to coach the Dark Blues, Leander and London Rowing Club. It was a busy schedule, but coaching remained his passion. In 1964 he was appointed as Head Coach of the Amateur Rowing Association (ARA), the national governing body for the sport of rowing. British rowing had been in the doldrums. The failure at the Rome Olympics of 1960 was not just a blip, Britain had failed to win an Olympic medal of any colour since London 1948. Gully Nickalls, President of the ARA, summed it up succinctly: 'British technique and equipment has failed to keep pace with the rapid developments overseas.'

Jumbo was seen as the perfect fit for Head Coach, someone who recognised the limitations of British boat and oar design but who could also get his crews to the peak of fitness and imbue a winning mentality, with the latest of technological gadgetry.

Jumbo's reign at British rowing was apparently to only last a few months. *The Times* broke the story on September 7th.

> 'A German professional coach is to be employed by the Amateur Rowing Association to take full charge of the national team after

next month's Olympic Games in Tokyo. He will supersede Group Captain H. R. A. Edwards'.

The ARA circulated a statement:

> 'We feel that if rowing in this country is to match the best that is produced on the Continent we must, at least in the early stages, be prepared to accept both their training methods and their coaching technique. In the course of time, we hope, it will be possible to take the best that the Continental clubs have to offer and to add to this the knowledge that already exists in this country; but in the initial phases of the scheme we feel it is essential to accept their teaching in full and without modification, until we can at least come somewhere near to matching their performance. With this object in view, we are endeavouring to obtain the services of a coach of standing and experience from Germany, and intend to hand over to him full control of the national team for at least the first year of its existence.'

For some in the rowing community, this was the most remarkable capitulation and admission of ineffectiveness ever to be published by a governing body of a British sport. For others, it was the dawn of realism, the first evidence of some degree of humility which was required as the prerequisite of learning anything from anyone.

The plans of the ARA were soon in disarray, and by November the Association confirmed that attempts to find a German professional coach to take charge of the British national rowing team had proved unsuccessful Jumbo was reinstated – but it was clear to all, especially to him, that the public attempt to secure the service of a German coach was not a vote of confidence in the direction that British rowing and the coaching was going. With reservations, Jumbo agreed to stay on for one further year.

There had been some success at the Tokyo Olympics of 1964. The coxless four had returned with a silver medal, but Jumbo had opted not to be part of the coaching team. Instead, with the ARA refusing to cover the

We Meet Again, Herr Krupp

Jumbo coaching his crew from the tideway on a megaphone that was gifted to him by the US Olympic team.

expense, Jumbo paid his own way to Japan to attend the training sessions and the regatta to make notes on the advances that the other countries had made to their technique and equipment.

In the 1950s – with Jumbo's rejuvenation of Oxford's fortunes – his 'art of rowing' coaching methods were innovative. The importance and centrality of fitness was ground-breaking and Jumbo's redesign of oar shapes and sizes gave his crews an added advantage. But by the mid-60s, evidenced by the ARA's desire to adopt German coaching techniques, Jumbo was beginning to be viewed as old fashioned.

The techniques that he had implemented had now been entrenched for years, and his morale-boosting tales of Athenians and Roman slaves rowing to battle, were not as inspiring as they once were. His drinking increased as his importance to British rowing began to wane.

Jumbo's fellow coaches would try to dissuade him from too much involvement in the latter stages of training, as he would tend to make changes that would often appear to be rash. Alcohol also provided a numbness to the guilt he felt over his brothers, his air crew, his friends, who all had died far too young. But his personal demons remained within himself –

The 1967 Oxford crew with Jumbo. This was the last time Oxford would win the Boat Race under the coaching of Jumbo. Dan Topolski (top row, right) would go on to coach Oxford fifteen times and faced his own mutiny in 1987.

a subject that he was unwilling to speak about, neither to his family nor to his boys in the boat.

Jumbo still retained respect. Robin Parish, who was coached by Jumbo in the late 1960s, recalled 'a superb technical coach, and a raconteur of glorious stories. I remember him coming into the changing room after an outing, when *The Times* or *Daily Telegraph* had commented on our weedy physique, and surveying us as we emerged from the showers: "I think you should know that you all have the physique of Greek Gods". Those *bon mots* echoed through one's psyche, as did other stories, at a time when ergometers were unknown. For me the romance of rowing and the feel of the boat running through the water was far more important than ergometer times or split 500s.'

John Dart, who was also coached by Jumbo in the 1960s, recalls that 'he was a character and much admired by us all for his achievements and his teaching of technique. I can still remember him on the river coaching in freezing weather in the heavy white "blanket" trousers and blue blazer in the launches *Bosporos* or *Nicea*, with Albert the boatman sitting ruddy-faced driving in the back.'

Tom Weil, who rowed for the Yale lightweight squad in the Thames Cup at Henley in 1970, recalled his first encounter with Jumbo. The Yale crew were quartered at a cottage near Henley and Jumbo was there in the garden relaxing with a large gin and tonic.

'I took the liberty of requesting Jumbo to inscribe my copy of *The Way of a Man with a Blade*. He had enjoyed a few drinks and consequently he did so with equal measures of grace and clumsiness. He started to sign under his frontispiece photo, but his unsteady hand ripped much of the page from its moorings. Undaunted, he then attacked the title page, with somewhat scrawled success. I offered profuse thanks, and retreated to the cottage, where I carefully taped the page fragment back into place. This mauled little volume is one of the most treasured association copies in my collection.'

The British Press were beginning to portray Jumbo as something like a jester from a Shakespearian play, adding light relief.

In a front-page news story with the headline 'Splash... Jumbo cycles into the river', The *Daily Express* gleefully informed its readers that:

'The Famous rowing coach took a dive at Henley Regatta yesterday – right over the handlebars of his bicycle into the Thames. Jumbo, pedalling furiously, megaphone in hand as he exhorted the London crew he coaches, overshot a corner. And Jumbo, megaphone, bike, and all, went in the drink with a mighty splash. Two policemen fished out the bike and Jumbo struck out for the shore. But just as he was being pulled out a woman yelled, "Your cap, it's floating away!" Jumbo spluttered, "My Goodness" and swam back to rescue his London Rowing Club cap. Later as he dried out in the Stewards' Enclosure and drank a gin and tonic to calm his nerves, he said "I must cringe here undignified until my blazer dries. But I can say I executed a most perfect swallow dive and that the water was commendably warm".'

Chapter 23

A Farewell to the Water

After leaving his coaching role at the Amateur Rowing Association, there would be one further adventure for Jumbo. In 1966, he entered the very first Round Britain and Ireland Yacht Race. Along with Wing Commander Jock Burrough, Jumbo crewed the trimaran *Tao* as one of the sixteen yachts that had entered this new sailing competition. *Tao* was owned by Burrough, but he handed over the role of skipper to Jumbo.

Starting and finishing in Plymouth, the course – of about two thousand miles – was split into five legs separated by compulsory stopovers of forty-eight hours each at Crosshaven in Ireland; Castle Bay, Barra in the Outer Hebrides; Lerwick in Shetland; and Harwich on the East Coast.

The trimaran of Edwards and Burrough started strongly and they were making excellent progress as they circumnavigated the British Isles. However, at the penultimate stop-over there was an almighty row between the two, and Wing Commander Jock Burrough sailed off without Jumbo.

For Jumbo this was a clear act of mutiny, and he reported it as such to the local police station.

In the official results of the 1966 race, there is the description next to the entry of *Tao*: 'Disqualified – finished with only one on board'.

Jumbo on his yacht Bosporos, *1970*

After this mutiny, Jumbo invested in his own yacht and had it moored on the Hamble river near Southampton. In honour of his happy memories on the river, he named the yacht after the Oxford coaching launch: *Bosporos*. When he was not coaching Oxford, or with Mike at their cottage, he would spend his days teaching sailing skills at 'The Jumbo School of Sailing'.

Whenever his grandchildren came to visit, they would have to stand on the pontoon and declaim quite sonorously 'Bosporos' and their grandfather would emerge from down below and row over in the rubber dinghy. The dinghy would be on the verge of sinking as Jumbo rowed back with his young passengers plus luggage.

Jumbo's last significant involvement in coaching a Boat Race crew was in 1970, when Cambridge won by three and a half lengths.

It was the end of an era. In total, Jumbo had been involved in coaching five Oxford crews to victory in the Boat Race.

Far more importantly, he had delivered to Oxford a restored pride in her rowing crews.

* * *

A Farewell to the Water

On Thursday, December 21st, 1972, the weather was cold and a mist hung low over the river Hamble. At sunset – as was his routine – Jumbo poured himself a gin and tonic and went out onto the deck of his yacht, *Bosporos*.

It had been forty years since he had returned to England with his two Olympic gold medals. The sun's rays weakly cut through the mist. The calm water of the Hamble reflected a brief golden hue.

As Jumbo sipped his drink, he looked out onto the water that he loved. The glass fell from his hand. He stumbled and collapsed onto the deck.

The last sound Jumbo heard was the gentle lapping of the water against the hull of his boat. He had faced death above the skies of Germany, and on the solitary grey expanse of the Atlantic, but this time there was to be no return. The battle was finally lost.

At the age of sixty-six, Group Captain Hugh Edwards bade a final farewell to the water that had defined his life.

Epilogue

Two days after Hugh Edwards died, on December 23rd, 1972, *The Times* published his obituary under the headline of 'An outstanding oarsman'.

> 'With the death of Group Captain H. R. A. 'Jumbo' Edwards, rowing loses one of its most colourful and famous personalities. He will be remembered as not only one of the greatest oarsmen of all time but also as a famous coach, innovator and raconteur. The loss of Jumbo Edwards to the sport will be grieved in almost every rowing nation of the world. His race record could only be described as phenomenal... Jumbo Edwards will be remembered as a successful boat race coach, particularly in the 1960s, and was chief coach of Oxford as recently as 1970. As a coach he was distinguished for his courage in experimenting and introducing innovations to the sport. The use of long oars, "spade" blades, methods of calculating wind and water speeds, calculating power output of oarsmen, specially designed boats and the use of interval training for conditioning oarsmen were all methods introduced by Jumbo Edwards in Britain in the pursuit of greater speed. He was not always successful with his experiments but displayed a rare courage in following his convictions, rather than slavishly copying other coaches and their methods. Jumbo Edwards was a trend setter in the sport. Edwards was above all, as a

coach, a supreme technician. Some felt that at times he was blinded with scientific aspects at the expense of other factors contributing to boat moving. Yet rowing experts such as Dr Karl Adam of West Germany often paid tribute to many of Edwards's theories. British rowing owes more to Jumbo Edwards than any other person in the sport as far as attention to the science of boat moving is concerned'.

Letters of condolence from friends and those who had rowed with Jumbo, or been coached by him, arrived for Mike over the following days. All the letters reminisced about the impact that Jumbo had made to their lives, both in and out of a boat.

Peter Coni (London Rowing Club) wrote down his memories of the man and coach:

> 'I seem to have been coached by practically all the highly rated coaches in England at some time, and I have always respected and thought more of Jumbo than of any of them, both for his coaching, but even more as a person. Of course he could be difficult, and unreasonable and infuriating at times, but his single mindedness and determination with his crews, and his personality as a friend, are things which are very rare, and which I shall always remember with love and affection.'

Ronnie Howard, who remained staunchly loyal to Jumbo during the mutiny in 1959 and who became Jumbo's protégé in coaching the Dark Blues, wrote emotionally:

> 'There can be very few people who could be owed so much by me. At a critical time in my career I put all my faith in Jumbo and his success gave me all the qualifications I have needed. I have always tried to model my coaching on Jumbo, not by repeating what he said but by thinking about it, developing my ideas, trying new things and using anyone else's good ideas just as Jumbo did. Jumbo could make one love him and work for him with blind confidence and he could also make one angry and determined to prove him

Epilogue

wrong. Of course Jumbo had his weaknesses which were partly the result of the strain which came from the extreme effort he put into his work. There are many who have said that he lost an awful lot of Boat Races for Oxford but these were the people who were jealous of the much greater number that he won'.

Tributes also arrived from those who had battled against Jumbo on the river. James Crowden, who rowed for and coached Cambridge in so many closely-fought tussles with Jumbo, recalled:

> 'Jumbo was a tremendous figure in the rowing world and all we Cambridge oarsmen had the greatest respect for him. He gave so much of his time so willingly to the sport we all love and his passing leaves a tremendous gap in the rowing world. I shall always cherish so many happy meetings with him and memories of battles on the river in the greatest sporting spirit.'

On March 12th, 1973, the memorial service for Group Captain Hugh Edwards was held in Oxford at Christ Church cathedral. William Rathbone, who had rowed with Jumbo and Sphinx in the 1926 Boat Race and had remained a close friend, delivered the eulogy. He recalled how he had to push Jumbo into an upright position after his collapse in the Oxford boat, but there was never a man more deserving of the glories that were to come his way at Henley and in Los Angeles.

In the packed cathedral, joining family and friends, were many mourners representing the rowing world and the RAF.

Jack Beresford and Felix Badcock regaled the men of that year's Oxford boat crew with stories of their great rivalry at the rowing clubs of Thames and London, and the glory of their Olympic gold in Los Angeles.

Group Captain Healy of the RAF spoke of Jumbo's bravery in the war, and of the countless lives saved through Jumbo's intense training of so many air crews.

Following on from tales of the war, Sir Charles Wheeler – friend and distinguished journalist – recalled with a smile, 'As an 8-year-old after seeing the Henley semi-final race against the Germans in 1931, I knew we should win the Second World War and that Jumbo Edwards would play a part'.

That Spring day in Christ Church Cathedral, within sight of the river, an extraordinary life was celebrated.

Hugh Robert Arthur Edwards DFC, AFC
1906–1972

Acknowledgements

It was in July 2017 when my father-in-law, David Edwards, asked me to write the story of his father's life. The two of us had spent the previous few years planning the structure of the book and approaching established authors who had experience in writing memoirs, but schedules and workloads were always obstacles. By July 2017, I had left full-time employment in the publishing industry and was working on setting up Lapwing Publishing Services. I had been commissioned to write a few articles for newspapers and websites on my research into sporting history and David had the faith in me to ask if I would be willing to take on the writing of this book. Without David's trust and belief in me as the author, this book would not have been possible. The sadness is that David did not live to see the publication of *Water's Gleaming Gold*. My hope is that David would have been proud of the final book and that the extraordinary life of his father has been faithfully told. When writing the chapters I always had David's voice in the back of my mind, conveying his wisdom about rowing techniques and military exploits. This book is dedicated to the memory of David, and his older brother John, who both forged their own extraordinary lives, not least as international oarsmen themselves.

Other Edwards family members deserve more than honourable mentions too. Jumbo's grandchildren Giulietta Horner, Bella Blanchard, Alex Edwards, Tarquin Edwards, Camilla Cañellas, Melissa Jamieson, and – sadly no longer with us – Charlie Edwards have all been central to the research, as has my mother-in-law Judy Edwards and John's widow Rosie Edwards. Their support, kindness and unfailing courtesy have all contributed so much to the writing efforts. Judy has also been so patient with my constant rummaging through the family archives, correspondence and photograph albums whenever we go and visit the house in Dorset. Having the use of the family cottage in Burnham-Overy-Staithe, Norfolk, as a writing retreat was also a haven of solitude. Walking along Holkham beach and across the marshes allowed me to imagine the Liberators and Blenheims setting off from the Second World War airfields on their way to missions over Germany and to patrol the North Sea.

The rowing community has been very patient with my regular queries and fact checking for the results of regattas and Boat Races. Foremost in their patience has been Göran Buckhorn, the founder of the rowing history website *Hear The Boat Sing* (www.heartheboatsing.com). Göran's advice and encouragement from the very first stages of the book, up to reading through drafts of the manuscript, has been invaluable. *Hear The Boat Sing* has been the online resource that I relied on the most for the very best of rowing journalism and research.

No author can survive without readers of the manuscript. Alongside my family, Peter Mallory - author of the 4-volume *The Story of Rowing*, and contributor to *Hear The Boat Sing* – has been so generous with his time in reading through the drafts. Thomas Weil has provided excellent feedback after reading through the proofs, whilst Chris Dodd and William O'Chee have helped immeasurably in my knowledge of rowing history.

John Beresford, son of the legendary Jack, invited me to his home in Gloucestershire and we spent a wonderful day looking through his father's photo albums from the Olympic Games. Several of the photographs from the Los Angeles Olympic Games were taken by Jack Beresford and I thank John and his family for allowing me to reproduce them in the book. John's memoir about his father, *Jack Beresford: An Olympian at War*, is also a wonderful read and it is apparent why Jack was such a heroic figure to Jumbo – ever since Jumbo's schooldays at Westminster.

Acknowledgements

Sheena Lawrence and Gay Sturt at Dragon's School have been so helpful with the history of the school and Christopher Seward was kind enough to read through the chapter about Jumbo's time at Westminster School.

Thank you to all those Old Blues and rowers who talked to me of their memories of Jumbo as a coach – especially Penny Chuter, Robin Parish, John Dart, Bill Rathbone, Jeremy Dale, David Badcock, Jock Mullard, Steve Wilmer, and the insights from the 1960 Olympians Dick Fishlock, Donald Shaw and Graham Cooper. For those wanting more insights into Jumbo's innovative coaching techniques then, if you can, do seek out his out-of-print book *The Way of a Man with the Blade*.

Estel Timofte, Research Coordinator at the Olympic Studies Centre in Lausanne, Switzerland, provided her time to look through the records from 1932 and to share with me the Olympic programme and rules book.

My research on the life of Lewis Clive would not have been possible without the assistance and kindness of the Clive family. Edward Clive and Charlotte Mitchell gave me their time and feedback on their great-uncle Lewis and read through the draft chapters. Tim Koch's excellent article on Lewis – and published on *Hear The Boat Sing* – was another excellent resource to consult. The partnership between Lewis and Jumbo was one of the most successful in the prestigious history of British coxless pairs, and research their achievements has been one of the main pleasures in writing the book. Their politics may have differed but, when they both got into a boat, they created an unbeatable partnership of talent and determination. If Jumbo's love of flying and Mike had not demotivated his passion of rowing, it would have been fascinating to have witnessed he and Lewis defend their coxless pairs Olympic title at Berlin in 1938 - in front of Adolf Hitler.

For Jumbo's years in the Royal Air Force, and especially his time with 53 Squadron, I was fortunate to discover that Jock Manson lived in the neighbouring town. As the historian of 53 Squadron, Jock graciously gave his time and expertise to assist me with the timeline of the squadron and the careers of both Jumbo and Sphinx. Jock patiently explained to me the various tactics used by Coastal Command in hunting down the U-Boats and protecting the vital Allied convoys. Pavel Turk was also able to advise me on the technical details of the Consolidated B-24 Liberator and it soon became apparent that Jumbo's escape from the sinking wreckage of BZ819 was nothing short of miraculous.

Through various online resources, I was able to track down the descendants of some of the aircrew that tragically lost their lives in the ditching of Liberator BZ819. They all kindly shared with me their family stories and found comfort in, finally, finding out the details of what happened on that November afternoon back in 1943. All the aircrew that died that day are commemorated on the Runnymede Memorial. Alexander (Alec) Davis, Jumbo's co-pilot, is also honoured on the excellent website *Remembering the Jews of WW2* maintained and edited by Cathie Hewitt. All of Jumbo's aircrew on that fateful mission were young men, in the prime of their lives, and it is important that their sacrifice is documented and remembered.

Through my research I also tracked down the family of Samuel Larner, the skipper of HMT *Lincolnshire* who rescued Jumbo from the Atlantic. Dai Larner, Samuel's grandson, sent through a copy of the letter from Jumbo's sister, Mona, thanking them for saving her brother's life. It was wonderful to read her words and to match this letter with the reply that Samuel had sent and that I discovered in our family archive of correspondence.

Marilyn Marrows Voullaire was able to share with me the information about her father, Dudley Marrows DSO, DFC. Jumbo and his aircrew helped to coordinate the rescue of her father and his Australian crew from the Bay of Biscay. Marilyn was kind enough to send me photographs of her father and his aircrew, one of which I have reproduced in the book with her permission.

For the chapter on 'Dark Blue Redemption', Teresa Stokes – daughter of Adrian Stokes – kindly provided me with her father's notes and recol-

Acknowledgements

lections of Jumbo, and with the photograph of the 1952 Oxford crew at Elstree Studios.

Many other writers have been kind enough to encourage me, console me and champion me. Thank you to Daniel James Brown, the author of one of the finest books on rowing: *The Boys in the Boat*. Dan's enthusiasm in the story when I first approached him gave me the impetus to write. My friend Richard Moore offered advice over several drinks when I first set out to write the book. Richard's books on cycling and athletics are amongst the finest examples of sports writing and it was devastating to all those who knew him and who profited so much from his generosity that he was taken from us so suddenly.

Tamsin McGee for a wonderful cover design and for her patience with all of my suggestions and late amendments.

To my ever-loving family, especially my parents who have always provided me with encouragement and a love of books. They both also painstakingly read through my drafts.

This book would never have got started, let alone finished, without my wife Melissa. Her constant support, encouragement and positivity with my writing endeavours never wavered – entrusting me to put onto the page the life of her grandfather. In those days when I was struggling with all the research and trying to find time to write, Melissa allowed me to escape to the solitude of North Norfolk for a few days and away from all distractions. On early morning winter walks over the sand dunes and along the beach, I reflected on our journey together ever since we first sipped our drinks beside the Thames at Henley Royal Regatta and the stories of Jumbo Edwards were first told to me. *Water's Gleaming Gold* is the end of that journey, but we have so many more adventures to look forward to.

Finally, my thanks and love to our daughters, Elysia and Liliana, the kindest and funniest girls I know.

A special heartfelt thanks to all those who contributed and gave their support to this book at its inception.

Robin Anderson	Jane Edwards	Adam Jolly
Anna Anderson	Judy Edwards	Rupert Jones
Edward Beard	Tarquin Edwards	Hereward Kaye
Sarah Blair Gould	James Elder	Michael Keillor
Jurij Benn	Annabel Falcon	Sergey Kochergan
Esther Bryan	William Fischer	Henry Law
Göran Buckhorn	Wendy Gomeze	Michele Law
Camilla Cañellas	Paul Gordon	Constantine Louloudis
Stephen Cobb	Matt Hall	Paul Loxley
Ruth Costello	Sarah Hastilow	John Machin
Edward Clive	Gill Hawkins	Roly Machin
Jamie Cunningham	Stuart Hawkins	James Manson
Jeremy Dale	Giulietta Horner	Tim Miller
Sarah Dean	Carl Husselmann	Jason McDonald
Fiona Eades	Ruth Husselmann	Tamsin McGee
Ross Eades	David Jamieson	David McLeish
Alexander Edwards	Patricia Jamieson	Elizabeth McLeish

Sandy McLeish

Richard Metcalf

Marcus Morrell

Ian Moss

John Mullard

Max Mumby

Catherine Parry-Wingfield

Maurice Parry-Wingfield

Douglas Paton

Alan Pattullo

Jason Payne-James

Sara Pearson

Jonathan Pegg

Katie Pryke

Simon Pryke

Marianne Rees-Hawkins

Christopher Seward

Marion Shave

Alyona Smith

Jan Smorczewski

Sylvie Spark

Anne Stevenson

Emily Stevenson

John Stevenson

Sam Stevenson

Corinne Stokes

Isabella Thun

Ally Underwood

Suzanne Underwood

Matt Weaver

Selected Bibliography

Beresford, John, *Jack Beresford: An Olympian at War* (The Cloister House Press, 2019)

Bird, Andrew, *Heroes of Coastal Command: The RAF's Maritime War 1939-1945* (Frontline Books, 2019)

Bourne, Gilbert C., *A Textbook of Oarsmanship* (H. Milford, London, 1925)

Bowman, Martin B., *B-24 Liberator 1939-45* (Patrick Stephens Limited, 1989)

British Olympic Association, *Official Report on the Xth Olympiad 1932* (B.O.A., London, 1932)

Brown, Daniel James, *The Boys in the Boat* (Pan Macmillan, London, 2014)

Burnell, Richard, *Henley Royal Regatta, A Celebration of 150 Years* (William Heinemann, London, 1989)

Burnell, Richard, *One Hundred and Fifty Years of the Oxford and Cambridge Boat Race* (Precision Press, Marlow, 1979)

Burnell, Richard, *The Oxford & Cambridge Boat Race 1829-1953* (Oxford University Press, 1954)

Campbell, John, *Royal Air Force Coastal Command* (Mereo, Cirencester, 2013)

Cross, Martin, *Olympic Obsession, The Inside Story of Britain's Most Successful Sport* (Breeden Books, Derby, 2001)

Dodd, Christopher, *Henley Royal Regatta* (Stanley Paul, London, 1989)

Dodd, Christopher, *The Oxford and Cambridge Boat Race* (Stanley Paul, London, 1983)

Dodd, Christopher, *The Story of World Rowing* (Stanley Paul, London, 1992)

Dodd, Christopher, *Water Boiling Aft, London Rowing Club, The First 150 Years, 1856-2006* (London Rowing Club, 2006)

Edwards, H.R.A., *The Way of a Man with a Blade* (Routledge & Kegan Paul, London, 1963)

Edwards, H.R.A., *Through the Usual Channels* (unpublished notes and recollections, 1971)

Fairbairn, Steve, *Rowing Notes of Steve Fairbairn of the Cambridge University Boat Club*, Edited by Arthur Eggar of First Trinity (Mills & Boon, London, 1926)

Fairbairn, Steve, *Some Secrets of Successful Rowing, including a system for training of a boat club and a exposure of the errors of 'orthodoxy'* (Sporting Handbooks, 1930)

Fairbairn, Steve, *Chats on Rowing* (W. Heffer & Sons Ltd, Cambridge, 1934)

Franks, Norman, *Dark Sky, Deep Water: First Hand Reflections on the Anti U-Boat War in WW2* (Grub Street, London, 1997)

Lehmann, R.C., *The Complete Oarsman* (Methuen & Co., London, 1908)

Mallory, Peter, *The Sport of Rowing* (River & Rowing Museum, Henley-on-Thames, 2011)

Manson, Jock, *United in Effort: The Story of No. 53 Squadron, Royal Air Force, 1916-1976* (Air Britain Publications, 1997)

Moore, Roger D., T*he 1932 Los Angeles Olympics: A Model for a Broken System* (Thesis submitted to the Faculty of the Graduate College of the Oklahoma State University, OH, 2015)

Nickalls, G.O. *"Gully," A Rainbow in the Sky* (Chatto & Windus, London, 1974)

Nickalls, G.O. & Mallam, Dr. P.C., *Rowing*, 2nd Edition (Pitman, London, 1952)

Nickalls, Guy, *Life's a Pudding, An Autobiography* (Faber & Faber, London, 1939)

Oldfield, Paul, *Victoria Crosses on the Western Front: Continuation of the German 1918 Offensives: 24 March - 24 July 1918* (Pen & Sword Military, Barnsley, 2019)

Page, Geoffrey, *Hear the Boat Sing, The History of Thames Rowing Club and Tideway Rowing* (The Kingwood Press, London, 1991)

Parkhouse, Gerald C., *Christ Church Boat Club, Crew Composition and Racing Results* (Christ Church Boat Club Society, Oxford, 1993)

Seward, Christopher, *In the Pink: A History of the Water at Westminster School Boat Club* (Self-published, 2023)

Topolski, Daniel, with Patrick Robinson, *True Blue, The Oxford Boat Race Mutiny* (Doubleday, New York, 1989)

About the author

Gavin Jamieson is a publisher, writer and researcher. After working in academic publishing for over twenty-five years he set up his own consultancy and imprint, Lapwing Publishing Services. As a writer and researcher he has contributed articles for the BBC, FC Barcelona, *The Guardian*, *The Scotsman*, *Hear The Boat Sing* and *ARA Sport*. 'Water's Gleaming Gold' is his first book. Gavin is a Director of the Cuckfield Book Festival and lives in Mid Sussex with his wife Melissa, their two daughters Ellie and Lili, and their cat Rocky.

Lapwing Publishing Services provides a hybrid publishing solution to produce books for authors to their own specifications at a realistic price as print-on-demand, or as a short or long print run.

With high production values and access to booksellers and online retailers, Lapwing will work closely with you to bring your manuscript to publication or to help with any publishing queries you may have whether it is fiction or non-fiction.

Visit Lapwing for more information:
www.lapwingpublishing.com